Call Her Blessed

. . . Every Woman Who Discovers
the Gifts of God

By

Lily M. Gyldenvand

AUGSBURG PUBLISHING HOUSE
Minneapolis   Minnesota

CALL HER BLESSED

Copyright © 1967 Augsburg Publishing House

All rights reserved

Library of Congress Catalog Card No. 67-11720

Manufactured in the United States of America

Foreword

In the 5th century B.C. Euripides, a Greek drama-tist, said, "There is no evil so terrible as a woman." It is difficult to know what experience gave rise to such bitterness in him, but obviously the wom-en in his life were something less than the ideal.

Another man, Lemuel, King of Massa, described a worthy woman in Proverbs 31, and what he wrote there he had learned from his own mother. "She is more precious than jewels," Lemuel wrote. She is ambitious, shrewd, clever, capable, wise, and has a sense of humor. "Her children rise up and call her blessed. The woman who fears the Lord is to be praised."

Woman's lot is not an easy one. Because her very nature is to give of herself, she is pulled in many directions by the loyalties that claim her. As a result she lives in the midst of terrific tension.

In these 52 meditations written by a woman for women, we take a good square look at ourselves to see the kind of women we tend naturally to be, honestly evaluating our many weaknesses and faults. Then we take a look into the Scriptures and discover there is meaning and purpose to life for the woman who depends upon the sufficiency of God. We discover that we have individual worth and dignity in the sight of God. Regardless of the circumstances of her life—be she wife, mother, widow, or single—the woman who fears the Lord is to be praised. Many shall rise up and *Call Her Blessed*.

Lily M. Gyldenvand

Table of Contents

Call Her Blessed

From Fig Leaves to Dacron

Fashion has come a long way since Eve used fig leaves to cover her nakedness. Over the years we have appropriated the hide and pelts of animals; we have taken the fragile filament from the silkworm's cocoon; we have separated the fluff from the seeds of cotton plants; we have woven linen from flax stems. Today's woman wears garments of chemically produced synthetic fibers which possess remarkable qualities of durability, soil and wrinkle resistance, and which bear such interesting names as nylon, dynel, arnel, and dacron. They are a vast improvement over fig leaves and almost as readily accessible.

Providing adequate clothing for ourselves and our families consumes a considerable proportion of our time and interest and it gobbles up a good share of the family budget. We consider clothing to be a basic necessity of life.

It all began when Eve disobeyed God. Sin destroyed the perfection and holiness in which she had been created and from that moment, in her own eyes, her very body became a shameful thing that she must hide. As heirs to Eve's sin, all succeeding generations have felt an instinctive need to hide themselves from the eyes of their fellow-men. In even the most primitive cultures some type of covering has been devised from grass or leaves. With the advent of civilization, wearing more clothing becomes almost a status symbol.

Clothing serves the primary function of covering nakedness, and it also can be a protection from the elements. Pride, however, has injected a third quality—personal adornment—into the matter of dress. To keep pace with rapidly changing styles and planned obsolescence makes us dizzy.

Once, modest fashionable people swathed themselves in many layers of heavy, cumbersome garments that must have been both inconvenient and uncomfortable. Today, however, the emphasis on casual living has reversed that tendency to the other extreme. People milling around any suburban shopping center give a distinct impression that modesty and decorum are no longer considered in the choice of apparel. Some of their outlandish and revealing outfits seem to have been concocted with the deliberate intention of creating a bizarre effect. Either this means they consider what they wear as unimportant or it signifies an unusual anxiety that their garb reflect what they consider themselves to be.

When Jesus warned against being unduly anxious about clothing, he called attention to the lilies of the field and the grass which God clothes with dignity and beauty. His illustration seemed also to say that we ought to be neither ostentatious nor eccentric in dress.

An admonition in 1 Tim. 2:9 is directed especially to women, "Women should adorn themselves modestly and sensibly in seemly apparel . . . by good deeds, as befits women who profess religion." Whatever her hairstyle, attire, or accessories, the Christian woman's emphasis ought to be upon the way she acts rather than upon what she wears. This is further amplified in 1 Peter 3:3, "Let not yours be the outward adorning . . . but let it be the hidden person of the heart with the imperishable jewel of a gentle and quiet spirit, which in God's sight is very precious."

Paul lists some qualities of personality that ought to be cast off as one casts off soiled garments: immorality, impurity, passion, evil desire, and covetousness. Then he added a few more dirty clothes that we will want to remove: anger, wrath, malice, slander, foul talk.

What she shall wear is not unimportant, nor is it all-important. The Christian woman may cover her nakedness with anything from fig leaves to dacron polyester. If it is "seemly," she need have no anxiety about it. Her real concern will be that her spirit is clad in the clean garments of compassion, kindness, lowliness, meekness, patience, and love. This is what really matters, for in the sight of God it is the spirit which is precious.

. . . *And So She Did!*

Remember the story of "The Little Red Hen"?

In the old nursery tale the little red hen, who shared quarters with a pig, a dog, a cat, and a duck, had some wheat she wanted ground into flour to be baked into cookies. She appealed for help from her friends but they didn't want to get involved, so they refused. Of course, each had a good excuse. The pig was in the middle of a mud puddle. The cat was too tired. The dog was busy—chasing his own tail. The duck's feathers were wet. If the job were to be done, the little red hen saw no alternative but to try to do it herself—and so she did! When the tantalizing aroma of the fresh-baked cookies wafted through the barnyard, everyone wanted a sample, but having withheld their services they had no right to enjoy the end result.

This may be a little farfetched, but it seems to be a picture of some church women, with the little red hen being the poor soul who has accepted responsibility as an officer. She sees a job that needs to be done, so she tries to enlist the help of the membership who elected her.

This diligent and conscientious officer calls one member after another, asking for their cooperation, but they all have excuses, some no more valid than those offered to the little red hen. Most of the excuses but thinly veil a basic reluctance to get involved. To her chagrin, the chairman finds that these women, who had pledged their support if she would only let her name be placed on the ballot, have virtually abandoned her.

Getting involved always costs something. It may mean an investment of time, effort, or sometimes even money. But we just don't want to be bothered. Many of us avoid involvement like the plague. The truth of the matter is that we just aren't willing to give anything of ourselves. So, like the little red hen, too often the chairman ends up doing the job all alone.

While the little red hen had no particular talent for grinding wheat or baking cookies, in the process she discovered a marvelous truth: she found she could do much more than she thought she could!

If we are willing to work and are faithful to our responsibilities, God will give us the ability, the strength, and even the time to do amazing things far beyond our expectations. To experience this exhilarating sense of accomplishment, we need only be willing to attempt great things.

If, however, we persist in finding it of greater importance to wallow in our own little mud puddles, to doze in the sun, to continue the futile chase after our own tails, or to give all our attention to our own wet feathers, we will miss the blessings of participation in kingdom work.

There are rewards for involvement which may not be immediately apparent. Women who willingly dedicate their service to the Lord in his church grow in grace and acquire skills that make all of their other burdens lighter.

We take the name of the Lord in vain when we call ourselves Christian and then shirk our duty as members of his body. The one thing the Lord demands of each of us is to be faithful.

"Who will help me grind my wheat?"

"I will," said the faithful church woman—and so she did!

Guaranteed Blessing

Have you ever been trapped by your own good intentions?

Moved by a generous impulse to respond to a need, you spoke up and offered your help in a specific way. Thinking about it later, you could kick yourself. "Why did I have to open my big mouth?" you ask yourself. Your subconscious self seeks desperately for an out, hoping for some good interruption or justifiable excuse that will get you released. But you just may have to follow through—especially if you have made your big gesture before witnesses! You are trapped by your own good intention!

It's so often this way with our good intentions. They come into being from a genuine compulsion to do good, to exert some special effort, or to spend some extra money unselfishly for the benefit of someone else. If that generous thought doesn't get expressed out loud, it very often gets squelched, sometimes by rationalization, "It wouldn't have been worth much anyway," or by procrastination, "Some day when I get time . . . ." Or the good intention may be quelled in a more subtle way. We think about it, letting our imaginations fill in details of just how it shall be accomplished, and soon we begin to think we have actually done the deed. We may even feel a sense of accomplishment—almost unaware that it is counterfeit—and we haven't done a thing except nourish and cherish a good intention!

Most of us aren't unduly ambitious. We do what we have to do. But the extras, those things not forced upon us by necessity or obligation, just don't get done. Especially if they don't show or won't reflect credit upon us.

Seeing an aged neighbor slowly pass the house with a load of groceries may stir a good intention. Next time I drive to the grocery store I will ask her to go with me or offer to do her shopping. It's a good and a genuine intention. It won't cost much extra effort, but next time I go to the store I am in a hurry, or maybe I just conveniently forget.

I noticed an especially clear Bible verse at circle meeting that speaks of Christian hope. I remember a friend who doesn't have hope, who is trying to earn her eternal salvation and who lives in constant fear that death will overtake her before she has done enough. I resolve that the next time I see her I will show her this portion of God's

Word with its assurance that when Jesus died for our sins he did a complete job. I determine to help her achieve the confident hope in Christ that I have. But when we next meet I've lost my courage, or I've forgotten my deep concern, or our talk flows into other channels of trivia. The moment is lost. Another good intention is aborted.

Dr. Samuel Johnson in 1775 made the classic statement, "Hell is paved with good intentions." An earlier writer expressed it a little differently, "Hell is full of good meanings and wishings," wrote George Herbert.

The Apostle Paul was concerned about himself in this regard. He wrote to the Romans, "I do not understand my own actions . . . I can will what is right, but I cannot do it. For I do not do the good I want, but the evil I do not want is what I do."

He recognized the perversity of human nature that tries to *do* things in the feebleness of its own strength. Paul complained that although his mind had good intentions, it was in conflict with his flesh which didn't want to do what his mind suggested.

But Paul found an answer. He said, ". . . in all these things we are more than conquerors through him who loved us." The only hope for us is to turn over our good intentions to the guidance, direction, and power of the Holy Spirit.

Thomas à Kempis wrote in his book *Imitation of Christ,* "If thou intend and seek nothing else but the will of God and the good of thy neighbor, thou shalt thoroughly enjoy inward liberty. When a man beginneth to grow lukewarm, then he is afraid of a little labor . . . but when he once beginneth to overcome himself perfectly, and to walk manfully in the way of God, then he esteemeth those things to be light, which seemed before grievous unto him."

Jesus told of a father who asked his two sons to work in his vineyard. The first son refused outright, but later relented and went to work. The second said that he would work, but he did not go out at all. Then Jesus asked the question, "Which of the two did the will of his father?"

In the matter of our evanescent good intentions, it becomes a matter of recognizing the will of God and then, by the grace of God, acting upon it.

If we are honest, we will have to admit that we often have to say, "I meant to . . . but I didn't do it." We have all offered to our Lord protestations of our supposed intentions. Had we better have offered less and at least have done what we said?

We prove to ourselves and to others the genuineness of our intentions by our actions. What we do is visible evidence of our love. Although love is an emotion of the heart, it is also a matter of the will. Jesus commanded us to love God and our fellow men with our heart and also with our mind and our strength. There needs to be a combination of the nice, warm, pleasant emotion with a dogged determination to do something about good intentions. The amazing result of the effort is that it kindles a warm, sacred glow of conscious affection for those whom we serve.

There is a guaranteed blessing for those who know what to do and then do it. Jesus made the promise and it is recorded in John 13:17, *If you know these things, blessed are you if you do them.*

Powerful Women

Power is not something that women normally covet or deliberately strive to achieve. But it is something they have, nevertheless.

It is an established fact that women control a large share of the nation's wealth; that they are the largest purchasers of consumer goods; that they create demands and set standards that give direction to industry.

It is acknowledged that women have tremendous potential in politics and that they can sway public opinion for or against any issue or candidate if they coordinate their efforts.

United for a common purpose, women can exert a strong, positive influence for good—or, if their goal is not worthy, the weight of their concerted action could be equally disastrous.

Women today have ever-widening interests. They are becoming increasingly effective in efforts to improve family and community life through intelligent and aggressive programs of activity in church and civic organizations. And they need this fellowship with other women and the opportunity to reach out beyond their own four walls to avoid a sense of futility and boredom that could blight their lives.

Women employed outside of the home have a somewhat broader base for their interests by reason of their work contacts. However, they too benefit from participation in an organic fellowship that extends their influence and concern beyond what could be purely selfish.

We ought to be aware of the strength we have in unity and with discretion and judgment direct it into channels where it will be of greatest benefit to society.

This power of joint action is one of the basic reasons for drawing Christian women together into organizations that support and undergird the missionary outreach of the church. In this way their drive and energy can be most effectively utilized in the ministry of concern.

As Christian women study their Bibles together, they begin to see themselves in proper perspective; they find Christian answers to life situations; they discover ideals toward which to direct their lives. They become aware of their basic nature as women and their basic capacity to love. They learn that they best fulfill their destiny by expressing love through service. The instinct to care for their own expands to supplying needs wherever they find them. A strong, mystical bond develops when women unite in a fellowship of concern. As they see the will of God revealed in his Word, they find means of doing it in an amazing demonstration of the power of unified action.

Any group working together for a common goal has great power, but even more tremendous is the strength of those who take their directive for action from the Bible. There they discover that through prayer they have access to all the power of the Holy Spirit and all the resources of heaven.

What good thing is there that cannot be accomplished by a dedicated group of powerful women?

Thaw and Let Rise

I had never tried to bake bread until I discovered the availability of frozen dough at the supermarket. It comes ready-shaped into loaves with instructions that sound disarmingly simple. All you do is *thaw, let rise,* and *bake.*

Let rise, the instructions said, but as I watched, that sodden heavy lump didn't seem to be making any effort in that direction. It should be in a warm place, the instructions suggested. So I put it into the oven which had been heated slightly. This was a mistake. Suddenly the dough expanded and filled with air so rapidly that it sagged frothily over the sides of the pan and hung there in quivering folds. Frantically I snatched it out of the oven, gathered the sticky mass together, plopped it onto a floured board, and began to knead and reshape it into a new loaf. Obviously I would have to *let rise* again—that is, if there was enough strength left in the leaven to perform a second time.

A half hour later the dough had lifted majestically, evenly, and firmly to a smooth, round dome, just the required one inch above the sides of the pan. It was ready to bake. When I took the golden loaf from the oven it was a thing of beauty. I felt a minor pride of accomplishment, even if all I did was *thaw, let rise,* and *bake.*

After this first experience with baking bread I think I understand a little better what Jesus meant when he said, "The kingdom of heaven is like leaven which a woman took and hid in three measures of meal till it was all leavened" (Matt. 13:33).

It takes only a very small amount of yeast to raise a quite sizable lump of dough. Yet this amazing power is not explosive. Even under pressure it won't "blow up." The worst that can happen is that it will become frothy, shapeless, and quite worthless. Leaven never lifts only one corner or one single spot. It lifts the whole thing, consistently, smoothly, and almost imperceptibly, but its influence is felt throughout the entire mass.

Yeast that is never taken from the package and mixed with the other ingredients doesn't perform its leavening function.

Christians living in the world are a part of the

kingdom of heaven. As such they are a leaven. If they are "active yeast," their influence will be felt as they mingle with the godly and the ungodly in their everyday experiences. They can steadily and gently change the atmosphere around them and lift the entire community to a higher level if the love of God is evidenced in their every contact with others. They will not "explode" under pressure, but they do have the ever-present danger that if they try too hard, their efforts may result only in a frothy puff.

We may sometimes be tempted to relax in the exclusive fellowship of other Christians who "understand one another." We may even avoid becoming involved in the affairs of our communities, as though we feared contamination by exposure to secular things. We act sometimes as though we don't believe our faith could stand to be challenged by anyone or anything with which we do not agree, so we withhold our participation and our Christian influence where it is most sorely needed.

If, as Jesus said, the kingdom of heaven is like leaven in a quantity of meal, then the Christian must come off the shelf and get mixed into the batter of life around him so that his influence can be felt.

We know the love of God in our own lives. We understand the necessity of forgiveness. We are convinced there is salvation only in Jesus Christ. We believe his redemptive power can transform people and circumstances. Therefore we must bring that Christian leaven into the political, cultural, educational, and social world in which we live.

How to Be a Success — Though Single

To you single women ("unclaimed blessings" someone has graciously dubbed you) there comes a time when you become aware that you are just about the last apple on the tree. One by one your friends have moved into the state of matrimony. You have been either hostess or guest at so many showers and you have bought so many wedding gifts you could have furnished a house. You've been a bridesmaid so many times your closet is jammed with dresses for which there is no right occasion. You have had so many bridal bouquets hurled at you with deadly accuracy that you feel slightly bruised. Even catching the nuptial flowers just never seemed to do the trick. You are getting a little weary of trying to find another bright reply to the perennial question, "How come a pretty girl like you isn't married?" Yet it is a fact of life. For one reason or another (and there are lots of excellent reasons) you are still single.

There are no dependable criteria for determining what predisposes one woman to spinsterhood and another to matrimony. And there doesn't seem to be any sure formula or any particular combination of assets which guarantees that every woman will find a mate. Certainly it is not true that only pretty women marry. A casual look around you will prove that in a hurry. Of course, the mass media advertisers have spread the propaganda that physical charm, especially when enhanced by a particular product, is the key that will open the door to marriage. But the reasons why one person will remain single and another will be married are far more numerous and more complex than that.

There is a measure of comfort in the statistics (which are very likely apocryphal) that for every single woman who wishes she were married there are seven married women who wish they weren't. We may say to ourselves (and mean it), "There are lots of things worse than being a happy old maid!" Yet not all single women can accept their lot with such apparent casual indifference. Too much of life is structured upon the presumption that everyone is married—or ought to be—and those who never make it are obviously failures.

Not too many years ago many households included a maiden aunt who was a sort of shadowy figure in the background of family life. She was handy to have around the house because she could usually help with the sewing and the housework. She was tolerated, sometimes grimly endured, perhaps respected, and occasionally loved. But she was not really part of the family. Fortunately, today most single women establish and maintain their own homes, support themselves, and live independent lives without the stigma of being the burden and responsibility of someone else.

But even in this enlightened age, success is too often equated with being married. Many single women feel the sting of defeat because they have never made the bride's journey down the aisle.

Naturally everyone wants to be successful. Everyone wants to achieve her highest potential. Marriage is, of course, a holy and desirable state that has been ordained by God and is blessed by him. The majority of women will, of course, marry, establish homes, and raise families. But some will not, and we are certainly deluding ourselves if we think that success in life depends upon our marital status. Being married is a circumstance of life and being single is another circumstance of life. How we relate to the particular circumstance to which each of us is called depends entirely upon the kind of person each of us is.

Whether married or single, our obligation as a child of God is to be a responsible individual, obedient to the laws of God and responsive to his love. God's formula for success is spelled out very clearly in Joshua 1:8, "This book of the law shall not depart out of your mouth, but you shall meditate on it day and night, that you may be careful to do according to all that is written in it; for then you shall make your way prosperous, and then *you shall have good success.*"

". . . meditate on it [the Word] day and night, that you may be careful to do according to all that is written in it." Then God assures success.

There is no reference to age, sex, or marital status in this admonition. It is addressed to the people of God.

The next verse gives added encouragement to all who would find this kind of success: "Have I not commanded you? Be strong and of good courage; be not frightened, neither be dismayed; for the Lord your God is with you wherever you go."

Written on Our Hearts

The TV news story shocked viewers with its gory pictures of injured children being dragged from an overturned school bus. What happened? The brakes failed.

In a world of wheels and high speed good brakes are extremely important. Without them there would be even more chaos, death, and destruction. Powerful things must have powerful and effective controls.

Human beings, created in the image of God with the freedom to select their own destinies, have latent power for either tremendous good or tremendous evil. We need an effective system of "brakes" in good working order for our own protection and for the good of others around us. A car driven without brakes is a menace, not only to the driver, but to everyone else. A man who does not curb his natural impulses endangers himself and others.

The civil laws of our country, as well as God's

moral laws, act as a curb for those who respect their authority. Our own consciences, especially when enlightened by the Word and the will of God, and our own good common sense, are "brakes" that can keep us from plunging head-long into disaster. Yet we must choose whether or not to use these available "brakes." We can ignore these safeguards, and we often do just that.

Our great goal in life is freedom. We chafe under restraint. We would like to shake off everything that restricts us. We want to shed our inhibitions; we try to muffle the weak voice of conscience; we find subtle ways of evading the stringencies of both civil and moral laws. We think if we could just get rid of all these things that hold us back we would be free. Yet we see what happened when the brakes failed.

The hardest thing for us to bring under control is our selves. Yet Jesus said, "Whoever will come after me, let him deny himself, take up his cross and follow me." The way of Christ is the way of self-denial. This means living under certain restrictions and within certain limitations. If we resent the implication that the Christian life puts some "brakes" on us, then we have failed to see that those "brakes" are necessary for our growth and for our own eternal protection. We grow by doing what is hard, by overcoming what is evil, by facing what is distasteful. If we do not deny ourselves and manage somehow to avoid all obligatory tasks, all unpleasant duties, all threatening ordeals, our character development is stunted. Christ's way, which asks for self-denial, self-control, and restraint within the framework of God's moral code, builds character.

The Word and the will of God ought to be so much a part of us that their "braking power" becomes almost automatic. This may be what the Psalmist meant when he wrote, "I have laid up thy word in my heart, that I might not sin against thee."

God's Law, which was formulated into just ten terse commandments, was further simplified by Jesus who said, "You shall love the Lord your God with all your heart, and with all your soul, and with all your mind. This is the great and first commandment. And a second is like it. You shall love your neighbor as yourself. On these two commandments depend all the law and the prophets."

It is the law of love which the God of Inner Discipline has written on our hearts and to which our conscience also bears witness (Rom. 2:15). Love—*Agape* love—as Christ exemplified it, is the most effective "brake." It is perhaps the only one powerful enough to control powerful human behavior. If that "brake" fails, there will be certain chaos, death, and destruction.

Who Will Roll Away the Stone?

The women knew they had a problem. If they had given much thought to it they might have been discouraged at the outset. But they didn't think about obstacles that morning. They thought only of their mission to bring spices and ointments as an expression of their love for a dead friend.

They were well on the way when one of them put it into words: *Who will roll away the stone?*

It is rather remarkable that even then they didn't lose heart and turn back. They resolutely continued on toward the cave where Jesus had been buried after his horrible, shameful death on Friday.

If the problem of rolling the stone from the entrance of the grave had kept them at home, or if they had turned back saying, "What's the use?" when it was called to their attention, they would have missed history's greatest moment—the declaration of victory to which the empty tomb was eloquent testimony.

There are many projected missions that come to nothing before they are even begun because anticipated problems loom so large they completely overshadow the venture.

Much good work that is begun with high hope and confidence loses the support of its most staunch promoters when someone gloomily calls attention to a roadblock ahead and points out that the detour around it will take too long or cost too much. How many glorious moments and tremendous opportunities have been missed because faith was not great enough to ignore or bypass obstacles!

These women, who kept their eyes on their goal and pursued their original purpose in spite of everything, were privileged not only to be the first to know that Jesus was risen, but as soon as they comprehended this tremendous fact they were commissioned to be missionaries.

"He is not here; for he has risen, as he said. Come, see the place where he lay. *Then go quickly and tell his disciples* . . . ," the angel said.

Their reaction was immediate—as it must be for anyone who comes to full assurance of the real identity of Jesus Christ. "They departed *quickly* from the tomb with fear and great joy, and *ran* to tell his disciples."

And then they got the extra bonus that gave them impetus as they ran with the message. A moment later they met Jesus himself on the path. It was a confrontation that erased any possible fragment of doubt. Matthew says that they "took hold of his feet and worshiped him."

The Jesus they had loved as a friend, the master they had served, the teacher from whom they had learned, they now worshiped as Lord, prostrating themselves before him in humility, as before God himself.

It is the nature of women to love and to serve those they love in selfless abandon. It is in the strength of their love that they accomplish fantastic things against overwhelming odds. With full confidence in divine intervention at the time of need, women who know Jesus have initiated and courageously completed some amazing missions. They have done it not by sheer physical strength and endurance but by the undefeatable combination of love, courage, and complete trust in God.

Who will roll away the stone?

We know, don't we?

If Only . . .

In evaluating the past, have you ever said, "If only I had done things differently" or, "I can never forgive myself"?

The beginning of a new year is a natural time to look at the mistakes and sins that are ugly blots on the record of the year just over. Remembering an old proverb that says, "Only a fool stumbles over the same stone twice," this might be a good time to resolve not to duplicate those wrongs in the year ahead.

Certainly we ought to regret past sins and foolish acts, but should we refuse to forgive ourselves for them? Can we justly withhold forgiveness from anyone—even ourselves?

In a moment of weakness Peter denied knowing Jesus. In misguided zeal Paul killed Christians and persecuted the church. Neither of them had pasts of which to be proud, but what if they had harbored their guilt and refused to forgive themselves? What if they had skulked through life thinking of themselves as second-rate citizens because of what they had done?

Peter's cowardice made him swear to a lie, but he asked for and received forgiveness from

Jesus. Although he must always have been sorrowfully aware of his faithlessness, he forgave himself. Later, on Pentecost Day, Peter, with conviction, told a congregation of thousands: "Repent and be baptized every one of you in the name of Jesus Christ for the forgiveness of your sins." He used his own experience of forgiveness as a building block to a stronger character.

Paul also knew the meaning of forgiveness and was convinced of the necessity of leaving the past in the past. He wrote: "Forgetting what lies behind and straining forward to what lies ahead, I press on . . . ." He suggested that a complete "about-face" to a new life is possible: "For just as you once yielded your members to impurity and to greater and greater iniquity, so now yield your members to righteousness for sanctification."

When Judas, on the other hand, realized the enormity of his crime against his Lord, it loomed before him as an insurmountable obstacle, impossible of forgiveness. Since he could not live with his sin, it drove him to self-destruction. While Peter and Paul used their mistakes and the marvelous experience of forgiveness as stepping-stones to better lives, Judas, whose sin was no more dastardly than theirs, let it engulf and destroy him.

It is a miracle of the grace and mercy of God that forgiveness is possible through Christ. The same miracle should give us grace to forgive ourselves and to change our lives. Paul explained it this way: "So that as Jesus Christ was raised from the dead by the glory of the Father, we, too, might walk in newness of life."

To dissipate energy in regret and to whine, "If only I had done things differently," doesn't change the past and gives no promise to the future. Only forgiveness can clear the record and give us a fresh start. If God can forgive us, certainly we ought to be able to forgive one another—and ourselves—and then go on from there in "newness of life."

Have No Anxiety

Anxiety is a vast, bleak emptiness that enshrouds its victims like a thick gray fog. Its cause is indefinite. It is formless, vague, and the more terrifying because it has no readily identifiable object.

Helmut Thielicke, in his book *The Silence of God*, contrasts anxiety with ordinary fear by stating that fear usually has a recognizable object.

We are afraid of *something.* Usually we know what it is. It may be a dread disease. It may be loss of a job. It may be some obvious danger. But being able to distinguish the thing we fear, there is hope. The threatening something may never materialize. There may be a cure. We may be able to correct the situation out of which the fear arises. Or, possibly, just plain good common sense caution may minimize the threat to the point of extinction.

When we are anxious, on the other hand, we may not be able to point to a reason. We may be filled with unreasoning panic and not know why. We may be engulfed by a silent nothing that threatens in a very real way, yet is elusive. We cannot grapple with what we do not know.

No one is immune to moments of anxiety. Even Jesus knew its awful grip when on the cross the weight of all mankind's sin cut him off from God. Sin always separates, for there can be no union of righteousness and unrighteousness. Peering into the vast empty blackness where he could no longer see God, Jesus cried in anguish, "My God, my God, why hast thou forsaken me?"

Anxiety will come whenever we allow sin to separate us from God. It does no good to rail at the darkness or to thresh about in frustration. Nor is there surcease in eating, drinking, or barbiturates. When anxiety sweeps over us we can take another lesson from Jesus. He refused the offered pain-killer (the wine mingled with gall) that would numb his senses temporarily but would do nothing to change his basic anxiety. Although he could not see God across that vast gulf which widened between them, he was confident that God was there and that God was attainable. His anguished cry was not directed into the empty nothing. It was addressed to God.

There are antidotes for anxiety. Paul listed them in his Philippian letter: *Have no anxiety about anything, but in everything by prayer and supplication with thanksgiving let your requests be made known to God. And the peace of God, which passes all understanding, will keep your hearts and your minds in Christ Jesus.*

"Anxiety is the broken bond—love is the bond restored," writes Thielicke. When we maintain contact with the Father through frequent communication, gratefully acknowledging his blessings, we reassure ourselves of his constant love. We need never experience anxiety at all if we let the peace of God which passes all understanding (and far surpasses the power of tranquilizers) keep our hearts and minds in Christ Jesus.

Here I Stand

It takes a special kind of courage to defy the established church. In fact, it must shake a dedicated member to the marrow of his bones to feel morally obligated to speak against his church. To ecclesiastical authority one ought normally to be able to give full confidence and respect. But when the church deviates from the truth, someone must be brave enough to speak.

Martin Luther stood virtually alone under the compulsion of a strong conviction that when there is a conflict between the Word of God and the doctrines of the church, God's Word must prevail.

"Here I stand, so help me God, I cannot do otherwise," he declared as he defiantly refused to recant. His courage was rooted in a sure knowledge of the facts. It was a reasonable, intelligent position based on understanding both sides of the issue. Had it been emotion, sentiment, or prejudice that motivated Martin Luther, he would have gone down in ignominious defeat.

"Here I stand, so help me God, I cannot do otherwise."

This is our heritage as Lutherans—that the Word of God is the final and only authority in all matters of faith, doctrine, and life. The Word alone, Grace alone, Faith alone. No perversion of the Scriptures should be tolerated by a true believer.

This is our heritage—yet how lightly we hold the things that this pioneer of our faith was willing to sacrifice his life to assure. We are easily blown about by "every wind of doctrine." We meekly back down under the slightest pressure. We knuckle under to the door-to-door missionaries who challenge us with false teachings. Why? Because we are so abysmally ignorant of the Bible truth!

We neither know nor are we much concerned about what the Word of God teaches. We really are not sure enough of the doctrines of our church or the shape of our own faith to be able to defend it on a scriptural basis. We are so eager to be pleasant and agreeable and so afraid of becoming involved in a religious argument that we readily agree to the basic good intentions of all religious faiths. We add our encouragement to the insipid generalization that since we are all headed toward the same place anyway, it really doesn't matter by which road we travel. *Doesn't it?*

However moral and righteous some teachings

may sound, if they do not show forth the God of the Bible as revealed through Jesus Christ; if they suggest some other way of salvation than through the vicarious death of Jesus Christ on the cross; if they minimize the authority of the Scriptures— then they are dangerous pitfalls to be avoided at all costs.

When challenged to defend our faith—and we often are—do we weakly concede that these apparently slight differences of interpretation are of no serious consequence? Do we go along with the concept that it doesn't matter what we believe as long as we are sincere? Or, like Martin Luther, will we have that special kind of courage that comes from a conviction of truth and an intelligent understanding of the Bible so that in calm assurance we can say, "Here I stand, so help me God, I cannot do otherwise"?

Ordeal or Vacation?

Little bundles of energy confined overlong in a hot car have explosive potential that can make traveling with children more of an ordeal than a vacation. But in spite of this, time away from the routine of home life can be a time of refreshment and renewal for both children and parents. In makeshift eating and sleeping processes can come a new sense of family unity. Flimsy canvas tent walls can create an illusion of solidarity and a cozy closeness that defies intrusion by the outside world. Living with some inconveniences in an informal atmosphere can reveal personality traits that may otherwise be unnoticed.

After two weeks of such unprecedented proximity, the father of two little girls told about some of the things they learned about each other. Among other things, he discovered that his two daughters reflected two distinct spiritual types. Intrigued by this, he sought and found scriptural justification for both views.

The first day out was hot. There was little relief from miles of endless driving to reach the campsite. The children were restless, asking repeatedly, "How much farther, Daddy?" They whined, begged for treats, and were generally obstreperous all day.

But they both knew they had been difficult. That night as they were being tucked into sleeping bags, each in turn asked God to forgive her behavior and each in her own way asked for a better day to come.

There was an interesting difference in their petitions. One prayed, "Lord Jesus, please make me be a good girl tomorrow." The other little girl, with brisk determination, declared, ". . . And I promise, Jesus, that I *will be* a better girl tomorrow."

While one of the children acknowledged her helplessness and asked simply for the grace of God to perform his miracle, the other, by a deliberate effort of the will, indicated her intention to amend her life by positive action. Since it is only by the grace of God that such an effort can be made, she was actually combining some personal grit with the grace of God.

The attitude of the little girl who simply threw herself and her problem upon the mercy of God might seem to be the right approach. That great promise, "My grace is sufficient for you, for my power is made perfect in weakness," substantiates the view.

But on the other hand, Scripture is full of admonitions that indicate the need for human participation in amending life situations. There are verses that suggest that we "live in harmony"; "live peaceably"; "run the race"; "put off the old nature"; and "put on the new." The Christian who recognizes the power of God also recognizes his own frailty by comparison. But the dignity which God has given to man in the freedom of choice imposes the obligation to *do* something. Thus the postulant deliberately chooses by specific acts of obedience and a positive exertion of his own effort to cooperate with the grace of God in bringing about the desired result.

Are you vacationing with your children this summer? They can teach you a great deal if you listen to them carefully. The simple faith of little children in the efficacy of prayer and their boundless energy for making new beginnings when one day has been spoiled are remarkable demonstrations of how the Gospel works to bring harmony and peace into life.

Before Daylight

He would have been a wonderful doctor! His natural compassion for suffering, his gentleness, his miraculous power to heal, all made him eminently qualified for the medical profession.

And the field was wide open. There was no competition for the endless supply of patients with divers diseases that would challenge the skill of any physician. Their suffering and need presented an appeal difficult to ignore.

But he walked away from it.

In the synogogue that Sabbath where he had amazed his listeners as he taught, he also had relieved a man of an unclean spirit which had plagued him for years. It didn't take long for news of this event to spread around the village.

Later in the day at Simon's home he found Simon's mother-in-law with a high fever. With a touch of his hand he healed her so completely that she arose from her sick bed, prepared and served a meal to her guests.

His reputation "spread like wildfire" throughout the entire area. Before evening the whole population of the town had gathered at the door, many of them ill and pleading for healing; many of them simply curious and looking for a further manifestation of this magic power.

He worked late that night, healing and helping the suffering. He must have been exhausted, and yet Mark records that in the morning he was up "a great while before day" and slipped away to a private and solitary place to pray.

Certainly the temptation was there to concentrate his attention and talents upon healing sick bodies. There was no doubt about the needs of these people. There were attractive rewards promised. His reputation was already well established. He would be sought after. He would have the personal satisfaction of achievement and the fame it would inevitably bring. He would "make a good living," and he would earn the lifelong gratitude of his patients. He would be engaged in a truly worthwhile occupation, doing much good for the people. But it wasn't enough.

The human Jesus must have been deeply touched by the physical suffering he saw. How could he walk away from the crying need that pressed upon him, clamoring for attention?

The divine Jesus saw a need much deeper and more urgent. He saw sick souls. If he allowed himself to be diverted from his dedicated task, the good he might do would be only superficial. He had been sent by God to do a greater work, to perform a deeper healing. And it would not win popularity for him. Human beings alienated from God are obsessed with their bodies. If something is wrong with them, they will search far and wide for a healer. They are not similarly disturbed by their spiritual health. They would prefer not to know all is not right with their souls and do not appreciate the suggestion that they need a deep inner cleansing.

But Jesus knew the will of God, and he was determined to do it despite the temptation to settle for something more attractive, less strenuous, more rewarding. So while the people slept, before daylight, he deliberately withdrew from the pressures that would dissuade him from doing the will of God so he could draw new strength, reinforce his courage, reassure his determination to do the will of God rather than simply to do good.

Can we who are human, but who have this identical purpose of knowing and doing the will of God, hope to accomplish it unless we, too, arise before daylight, if necessary, to be alone with God, so that we may be filled with his power for whatever task he has set before us? What Jesus left undone to do his uniquely appointed work, may be within God's will for us.

About Our Father's Business

His words were a rebuke. He seemed surprised that his mother was not aware of the obvious— that he must be about his Father's business.

He was an adolescent, only a boy of twelve,

but he had reached the time when he must make the first cut in the tie that bound him to his human family.

The child, sooner than the mother, recognizes the time when he must assert himself as an individual. Mother love could easily become smothering possessiveness unless he did. Of course, he is not ready to be "turned loose" upon his own when he makes his first tentative gesture toward independence, but he is outgrowing the need for full-time parental supervision and is ready to be trusted to do some things and make some decisions entirely by himself.

When this time comes, it cannot be without some heartache for Mother. For several years he has been her major concern, her life, her work, her purpose and objective. During these years she has felt fulfilled and needed. Suddenly he no longer really needs her and is anxious to cut the ties. That Mother should feel bereft is not surprising. But she is up against a fact of life. She must begin to relax her hold on her child.

The cord between Jesus and his mother was cut with decisive finality at the wedding of Cana. Now he was a full-grown man, ready to begin his special ministry. He could no longer take direction from his mother, nor could he be swayed from the singleness of his purpose by his love for her. The break must be clean and complete

"O woman, what have you to do with me?" he asked, and he did not even call her Mother. Almost coldly he shrugged off her suggestion of what needed to be done.

Does this disturb you, Mothers? Does it seem lacking in even proper respect for the one who bore him, raised him, loves him? Then remember the conditions of discipleship (Matt. 10:34-39) which include this: "He who loves father or mother more than me is not worthy of me." His love for his mother must not dissuade Jesus from his obedience to God. Mary had to learn this, and it was a hard lesson, as it must be for any mother whose child must shake off her instinctive desire to protect him indefinitely.

Every child must find his own identity. He must be permitted to stand as a responsible individual before God, poised and ready to do his bidding without assistance or interference from others—even Mother.

When the time comes that Mother's job is done there may be a void in her life. Aware that her child does not need her in the same way any longer, she may collapse like an empty shell unless she realizes that she, too, is an independent person with her own obligation to God. She, too, must be in her Father's house. She, too, must be about her Father's business. His business can sustain any woman in peace and happiness and especially when the child she has reared according to his will has left her to live his own life in obedience to his own calling from God.

Hidden Treasure

He was a most unlikely choice—a common thief—but Jesus saw something in him others didn't recognize.

Before he left, Jesus made arrangements to meet him later that day. It was a definite date and no doubt the meeting actually did take place. And there must have been great jubilation at the time, for there is always joy in heaven over one sinner who repents.

The thief, paying for his crimes on a cross, recognized that the Man who hung beside him was a real King. He asked only to be remembered when Jesus should reach his kingdom. Not only would he remember him, but Jesus made a date with him. "Today," he said, "you will be with me in Paradise."

Jesus had a propensity for choosing unlikely friends. He was accused of surrounding himself with drunkards and social misfits. It was strange, however, that these ultimately proved to be inspired selections. Jesus seemed to sense hidden qualities in people that were not obvious to casual observers.

Unlike most of us, Jesus did not worry about how his own social status would be affected by the people he befriended.

Certainly he picked a motley bunch of unpolished, untrained men and designated them to carry his vital message to a world-wide audience. After all, the cause of the Christian church depended heavily upon them. We would have sought out well-qualified, highly educated men with strong personalities, good appearance, and proven skill in salesmanship and organization. Fortunately, selection of the Apostles was made by One who understood people!

Who would have guessed there was virtue in Mary Magdalene? Jesus did. He knew, however, that first she would need the cleansing of forgiveness and then the hidden qualities of her personality would emerge. She would never have been approved by a mission board, but Jesus chose to send her out to "Go and tell Peter and the others." An unlikely missionary? Perhaps, but she carried the truth with conviction!

In a current election, the man most likely to succeed is the candidate who makes the best television appearance and exudes the most personal charm. His opponent may have a better platform and more real ability for the job, but voters are apt to give their support to the one who makes the best outward impression.

The self-assured lady in the mink stole has a better chance of being chosen to lead women's activities than the little fat lady whose slip always seems to show under an uneven hemline. The "mink lady" may or may not be better qualified for leadership, but her grooming may be the determining factor rather than her dedication to the cause, her compatibility, or her ability.

If we give people a chance, we may discover and reveal some amazing hidden treasures of personality. Opportunities for growth and development are too often accorded to certain people for purely superficial reasons. If we could only see each other as Jesus sees us, perhaps we would not so often make judgments on mere externals.

Looking at people with eyes of love as Jesus did, we may see goodness, consecration, and loyalty that has never been encouraged. Some of the least likely people might be able to give valuable service and cooperation if they were only given a chance to be used.

Though it may be obscured, there is goodness in all people. Jesus set an example for us in this matter, too. He always looked beneath the surface, and as a result he discovered some remarkable qualities in some seemingly unremarkable people.

Look around you! There may be some hidden treasures of personality that will turn out to be real jewels if we make the effort to unearth them!

Don't Count the People!

If you have even a grain of compassion for suffering people, you will sense an almost overwhelming helplessness when you read the day's news and let it speak to you of the millions who are living in whatever rags they can find to cover themselves, who wander homeless, seeking any refuge from the cold, who are gradually dying from starvation.

To become acutely aware of these social injustices to fellow human beings and to comprehend how fantastically many people are thus victimized, and then to try to relate yourself and your ability to help the situation, cannot but leave you frustrated.

How can we possibly provide enough food to combat such gigantic hunger?

How can we possibly produce enough clothes to cover all that nakedness?

How can we possibly build adequate housing to shelter all the displaced people who now huddle in makeshift hovels?

How can we possibly bring effective economic assistance to nations where political raiders under the guise of friendship have come to loot and have then abandoned them?

How can we possibly exert a positive Christian influence upon spirits already so demoralized by the evil they have experienced that they no longer can believe in anything so seemingly ephemeral as love?

There are just too many people! The job is just too big! What we can do is but a drop in a bottomless bucket.

The alternative to this frustration is to shrug our shoulders, quell the disturbing emotion of sympathy that these startling facts have aroused, and take a measure of comfort from the assurance that we truly are of all people most blessed. Since we can't put a dent in the world's suffering, why try? We might just as well relax and enjoy our plenty. Very cleverly the devil has turned sympathy to frustration and then back into its customary inertia!

The disciples of Jesus were moved to compassion for the multitude who followed Jesus into the mountain to hear him preach. It was dinner time and no arrangements had been made for food. But the disciples' sympathy for the hungry listeners quickly turned to helpless frustration. How could they possibly feed all these people? Their progressions toward inertia, however, was brought up short when Jesus, in effect, said to them, "Don't count the people . . . count what you have."

He turned their attention from enumerating the people to inventorying their resources, but it was so little—only a few loaves and fish—that they turned anxiously to the Master.

What happened? Jesus in calm confidence gave thanks, asked God to bless the little bit of food, and amazingly it increased as it was used so that all were fed and there was even a surplus to be gathered up when the meal was over.

"Don't count the people," Jesus is saying to us

today, "for that will lead to despair. Begin with
what you have, thank God for it, and he will give
the increase."

"God's almightiness is limited only by man's
willingness." Our refusal to put even our meager
possessions at his disposal keeps people hungry,
naked, and destitute the world over. Don't count
the people, count your blessings—and miracles
of God will happen!

Baby-Sitting With Jesus

It isn't easy to explain death to a small child—
especially when it is the departure of a much-
loved grandfather whose delight had been frequent opportunities to baby-sit with his grand-
children.

However, the simple statement: "Grandpa has
gone to heaven to be with Jesus" satisfied, and it
was happily accepted with the casual comment,
"Now Grandpa can baby-sit with Jesus."

This child knew Jesus from a picture in her
room of the infant with his mother. So warm and
real was her feeling for the familiar Child that
she was willing to share her own favorite baby-
sitter with him.

A limited concept of the divine personality is charming in a small child. It is sheer tragedy when an adult comprehension stops at this level.

To keep Jesus in swaddling clothes would make it unnecessary to heed the persistent demands his mature manhood imposes upon us.

Who can see him meet and defeat temptation without shame for his own inability to resist an enticing lure?

To keep Jesus helpless in the manger crib is to evade responsibility for his compelling mandate to reach into far and uncomfortable places to teach and preach.

Who can see him lifting, healing, and helping the diseased, depressed, the dirty, and then justify a revulsion for contact with the sorry people of the world?

To keep Jesus cooing in his mother's arms is to close our ears to the utterly despondent, piercing question of a man suspended between heaven and earth: "My God, my God, why hast thou forsaken me?"

Who can look upon that broken figure, violated by all the indignities man can inflict upon man, and be untouched by horror and guilt?

To keep Jesus the lovely Child of Christmas with whom it might be a pleasant diversion to baby-sit is to draw a curtain on the brilliance of that morning when he defied the finality of death.

Who can view this triumphant Son of God and not in trembling awe bow in the presence of unquestionable majesty?

To love a baby with its sweet natural appeal is easy.

To love a fanatic with offbeat revolutionary ideas is not so easy.

To love a dirty, bruised, and bloody man who has been publicly condemned is extremely difficult.

God wanted his Son to be comprehensible to all sorts and conditions of men, so he was exposed to life and death as all men are.

We love the infant. We follow the young teacher. We suffer with the persecuted one. We worship the Son of God.

We must be disciples—not baby-sitters!

In Favor With God

In the scriptural account of the maturing of Jesus, it states that he grew in wisdom, in stature, and *in favor with God and man.* Thus do all normal people develop: intellectually, physically, spiritually, and socially.

There are people who have fully developed bodies and dwarfed minds. Some have brilliant intellects in underdeveloped bodies. Some are physically perfect with good minds, but they are spiritual pygmies, having entirely neglected their spiritual growth.

It is not enough to grow tall or to develop intelligence. The full-grown adult must also grow up both spiritually and socially.

There is a direct relationship between our spiritual and our social maturity. How we get along with people is one evidence of how we get along with God. Both are contingent upon the measure of our love: of God and toward others. We love (others) because he (God) first loved us. If we have not recognized God's love for us, we may not have begun to reflect it toward others. If we have a resentment toward the Creator, there is likely to be a resentment toward his other creatures. Thus we may be underdeveloped in these two important areas of maturity. If we are out of harmony with God, it is difficult to establish a good, healthy social climate with others.

Social contacts are necessary because of the individual's need for the support and encouragement of friends and his fear of loneliness. If the rights and privileges we claim for ourselves are not to infringe upon those of our neighbors, there must be tolerance, understanding, and a mutual consideration of one another at all times.

The best possible atmosphere is established between people when consideration, motivated by love, is manifested by both parties through personal control. This means self-control, control of tongue, temper, emotions, and appetites. Allowing any of these to run rampant without restriction, guidance, or direction is to guarantee disruption of community fellowship.

Like all other processes of maturing, getting along with people requires some effort on our part. Since we do not come equipped with automatic control mechanisms, this means much self-discipline.

To grow in favor with man is a mark of Christian maturity and a most desirable thing. World peace begins not with nations but with individuals who reflect the love of God and who respect one another enough to strive toward a good social relationship through controlling these qualities of personality that determine what kind of people we are.

Taken for Granted

Relentless rain during the night added to the already swollen rivers whose banks could no longer contain the rushing water. A devastating flood moved rapidly toward the center of the city.

Confident that I would soon be out of the danger area, I observed the phenomenon calmly and set out to claim my plane reservation back to Minneapolis. En route to the airport the civilian police stopped us. The field was flooded and all planes were grounded, they said.

No matter, I thought, I would take a train. But washed-out bridges to the north had cut off rail service. I inquired about a northbound bus, but again had no success, for deep water, missing bridges, and hazardous driving had brought them all to a halt.

Still I was not too disturbed. I would simply call my office, advise them of my dilemma and return to the hotel to wait it out. But the telephone lines were down and telegrams could not be sent either. In the brief time since I checked out of the hotel, water had surrounded it and covered the first floor.

Suddenly I wanted desperately to escape. I knew now that none of the taken-for-granted transportation or communication conveniences was available to me. Had I ever properly appreciated them and the prompt, efficient service of the past? I'm afraid I had not. They were just there, available when needed. I hadn't given any thought to being grateful for them. If I could pay for service, they could always perform—before, that is!

There are other vital commonplace things we take for granted. Do we really appreciate the air that surrounds us? If not, perhaps we have not seen people in hospitals buying one more breath in anguish, when a lungful of fresh air is all that stands between them and death.

The blood coursing through our veins on its appointed rounds; the amazing network of bones, muscles, nerves; the coordinated precision with which these mechanisms function—these are certainly not common things. These blessings of God make each individual human being a self-contained powerhouse of intellectual, spiritual, and physical energy. Yet we take these marvelous bodies, God's miracles of creation, for granted! We assume that they will continue to operate efficiently with no disruption in service, ready to spring into action whenever we call upon them to perform.

I was lucky. I got a seat on a southbound bus, the last bus to leave town over a bridge that the authorities hoped would not give way. Even though the bus was going in the wrong direction, I eventually reached home.

The lesson of this experience was clear: none of the blessings of life ought ever to be taken for granted!

How Did I Get Into This?

So you couldn't think of an excuse quickly enough to get yourself off the hook when the nominating committee called?

Now you're stuck with a job that looks a little overwhelming. Perhaps you are asking yourself: Who do I think I am, promising to tackle this big job? Things will really flop if they depend on me for leadership. How can I squeeze in all this extra work? I just can't do it! I have neither the ability nor the training for such a responsibility. I'll be so nervous. How did I get into this? I wonder if I can still wiggle out?

A little "stage fright" is natural and healthier by far than a cocksure confidence that you are the best and only woman for the job.

A far more Christian attitude toward any assignment, however, is to recognize that you have been called—not by a group of women looking for a "sucker" to do all the work—but you have been called by God with an invitation to participate in his important work.

No one knows your talent and educational deficiencies better than you do, but while you may honestly acknowledge your lack, if you are willing to be used, you will soon learn, as Paul did, the amazing truth that God's strength is made perfect in your weakness. If you willingly dedicate yourself just as you are to the task to which you have been called, it is possible to admit to human frailty and still with complete assurance echo Paul's words: "I can do all things in him who strengthens me" (Phil. 4:13).

The secret is simply to quit dwelling on your own inadequacies and keep your attention riveted upon the all-sufficiency of Christ. It is his call to you to do his work, and he has promised to give you the ability and the strength to do it. Your effectiveness in the job is qualified only by your willingness to serve.

One day Jesus called Peter. Without enumerating his talents or evaluating his ability, Peter responded. Now, anyone knows that it is contrary to the laws of nature for a man to walk on the water—but Peter didn't give that a thought. He heard the Lord's call and willingly responded. Amazingly, he got along just fine until he took his eyes off Jesus when he became aware of the boisterous wind. Suddenly he was conscious only of the danger of this strange and seemingly impossible thing he was doing. It was only then, when he began to think of himself and sensed the external pressures, that he began to sink.

We can do equally fantastic things when called by Jesus to do them if we look to him for direction and depend on him for strength. Like Peter, if we fear the wind of criticism that may blow wildly around us, or if we let the sense of our own frailty overwhelm us, we, too, will sink.

Scripture is full of promises from God to supply the needs of those who do his will, but it also has a number of admonitions for the conduct of the servants of God. One that all should heed who have an assignment in the kingdom is found in 2 Tim. 2:15, "Do your best to present yourself to God as one approved, a workman who has no need to be ashamed, rightly handling the word of truth." We may accept a call being fully aware of our lack of ability and training, but having assumed the responsibilities of it, we have an obligation to study hard, work hard, and strive to improve our skills and techniques.

"How did I get into this?" You may not be quite sure how you happened to be selected, but if you willingly accept, trust the Lord to provide, and work at it, you will realize that *it's a privilege!*

Allergic to Personalities

"I just can't stand Mrs. So-and-so!" Have you ever heard this comment? Have you ever made the comment yourself?

In all honesty, most of us must admit that there are people we find "hard to take." There are people with irritating personal characteristics that seem to rub us the wrong way. For reasons we can't always pinpoint, they irk us. At every contact our personalities seem to clash. This "allergy to personalities" may not bring on a fit of sneezing or cause us to break out in a rash, but it is a serious illness nevertheless.

A doctor, in trying to isolate the cause of allergic reactions, makes what is called a "patch test." This helps identify the factors that cause an adverse reaction. The careful physician, however, would not neglect a thorough examination of the patient himself to ascertain whether the trouble may possibly come from within rather than from some external irritant.

In this matter of a possible "allergy to personalities," a little self-examination might also be in order. It is entirely possible that the fault does not lie entirely with the other person.

Am I irritating to him, too? Does my attitude of critical superiority give him such a feeling of inadequacy that he must compensate with a show of bravado and boasting?

Does my thoughtless unkindness trigger an automatic reflex of harshness and vengeance from him as a measure of self-preservation?

Are my adversary's annoying personality traits simply a bid for attention because I have contributed to his feeling of social insecurity? Have I ever done anything that would bolster his self-confidence and assure him of understanding and encouragement?

Is it possible there are pressures in his life that I do not understand because I've never taken the trouble to open a sympathetic ear?

Do I dare extend a gesture of friendship, or will I just get more deeply involved with someone I have already decided "I just can't tolerate"?

Have I overlooked some opportunity to reinforce his courage with some honest compliment that I can offer him in all sincerity?

The cure may require the grace of God to endure, to overlook, to humbly apologize. It may require some personal grit to overcome a deep revulsion or to conquer a prejudice. The grace of God, which can mellow the spirit and change attitudes, combined with determined effort to correct an intolerable situation, can effect a cure.

Make the "patch test" to determine just what is causing your irritation, but also, by all means, make a thorough self-examination, too. Just plain unadulterated friendliness, liberally applied, may bring the desired results!

Lucky, Lucky, Load of Hay

As children, whenever we saw a horse-drawn load of hay, we considered it a lucky talisman and would hastily intone the magic words: "Lucky, lucky, load of hay; make a wish and turn away."

To take a second look at the wagon would break the charm and bad luck would inevitably follow. If the horses happened to be white, however, the sign was especially favorable.

We also religiously saluted the first evening star with the chant: "Star light, star bright, first star I see tonight, wish I may, wish I might, have the wish I wish tonight."

Another carefully observed ritual was "pulling the wishbone" after a chicken dinner. When the wishbone had reached the proper degree of brittleness in the warming oven of the kitchen stove, we would each grasp a prong and pull, concentrating hard on some cherished wish. If the bone broke with the round flat center piece on the side you held, you were assured your wish would be granted.

Blowing out all the birthday candles in one breath was another tried and proven method of achieving childhood desires.

Many adults advance far into maturity still carefully observing superstitious taboos and doing obeisance to the capricious Lady Luck.

Wishing is a passive escape from reality, with an opiate effect that helps us forget who and where we are. In this upsurge of longing for something better, hard reality dissolves into the bright world of imagination. But there would be little progress if there were no dreamers who wish to improve their lot in life. Legend has it that it was a lazy man with rebellious muscles who first conceived the idea of the wheel which launched the age of industrial civilization. However hard we wish, unless sufficient energy is applied to it, a wish is a vapid thing that dissolves into nothing as easily as it appeared.

In all people there is an instinctive outreach for the blessing of some unseen power—be it luck or some lesser god. For many, unfortunately, this is the sum and substance of their religion.

The Christian, who knows the Word of God and has learned the power of prayer, need not resort to chicken bones or loads of hay to invoke the blessings of God. God is not coy that he must be wooed. He does not require charms and chantings to gain his favor. We need not fear that a misstep in the prescribed pattern of worship will spoil our chances with him. He does not delight in sacrifices or burnt offerings, but "the sacrifice acceptable to God is a broken spirit; a broken and contrite heart . . ." (Ps. 51:16).

Among the wonderful things which he has promised are the means of making our wishes come true:

Unlimited Ability. "I can do all things in him who strengthens me" (Phil. 4:13).

Necessary Resources. "My God will supply every need of yours . . ." (Phil. 4:19).

For what more could one wish?

I Who Speak to You Am He

Three women came to Jesus with big problems.

One was identified in Scripture simply as "a woman who was a sinner."

One was gravely ill, having hemorrhaged for twelve years.

One had a daughter who was demon-possessed.

Three problems: spiritual, physical, and mental-emotional. In each instance Jesus disposed of the problem and then commended each of the women for her faith.

To the sinner he said, "Your faith has saved you. Go in peace."

To the sick woman he said, "Your faith has made you well. Go in peace."

To the woman with the troubled daughter he said, "O woman, great is your faith. Be it done for you as you desire."

In three other incidents when Jesus had an encounter with a woman, the matter of his real identification was of primary importance. Once this was established, there followed a declaration of belief in him. This newly discovered knowledge was communicated to others. The results were not the same in all cases.

One woman, a stranger to Jesus, was a Samaritan whom he met at a well on one of his journeys. At first she thought him to be a prophet because he knew all about her private life. Listening to him a little more, however, she confided, "I know that Messiah is coming (he who is called Christ); when he comes, he will show us all things."

At this point Jesus identified himself, "I who speak to you am he."

She believed and her reaction was to go at once to tell others. The result: "Many Samaritans from that city believed in him *because of the woman's testimony.*"

The second woman was Martha, an old friend, the sister of Mary and Lazarus. At first she began to berate Jesus because he had not been there earlier. But Jesus stopped her. It was more important that Martha should know right then who he really was. He said, "I am the resurrection and the

life, he who believes in me, though he die, yet
shall he live. . . . *Do you believe this?"*

Then Martha, at last understanding that Jesus
is the Lord of life and death, made her confession,
"Yes, Lord, I believe that you are the Christ, the
Son of God, he who is coming into the world."
There were others present who heard this and
who saw Jesus miraculously bring Lazarus back
to life. The result: "Many of the Jews therefore
who had seen what he did, believed in him."

The third encounter was with a woman whom
Jesus had befriended when she needed help. In
a dramatic meeting early on Easter morning, Mary
Magdalene first mistook him for the gardener. But
then she was given full comprehension of his
identity. In the moment that she recognized him
as her risen Lord, she fell on her knees in faith.
Immediately Jesus asked her to go and tell the
disciples.

It is interesting to note that the disciples did
not accept her witness. Luke records, ". . . but
these words seemed to them an idle tale, and
they did not believe them." The disciples had to
see for themselves before they would believe.

Have you had an encounter with Jesus? Has he
forgiven your sin, or healed your body, or restored wholeness to one of your loved ones?

Do you know who he is? Do you believe he is the Christ, the Son of God? Then what have you done with that knowledge and that faith? Have you communicated it to someone else?

Whatever else transpires in an experience with Jesus, the important result must be that you know for sure who he is and that you believe. If you do, then, like these other women who met him face to face, you will not be able to keep silent.

Who's Afraid?

Who's afraid? Well, the chairman of the meeting for one. She was pale as she stood before the group. The notes in her hand trembled. A vein at her temple throbbed visibly. When she began to speak her voice quavered slightly. She was short of breath and the words didn't come out quite right. But she plunged ahead and bravely brought the meeting to order and introduced the guest speaker.

Her courage had vastly improved by the time she returned to the podium to conclude the meeting. She seemed almost gay—perhaps because the ordeal was just about over, but perhaps also because she had a subtle sense of accomplishment in having faced a difficult job and having done her best with it.

Who's afraid? Moses was afraid when God singled him out for a special task. The prospect of going to Egypt on God's business terrified him. He was full of excuses:

"Who am I that I should go?"

"What shall I say to them?"

"They will not believe me or listen to my voice."

"I am not eloquent. . . . I am slow of speech and of tongue."

After having disparaged himself and having complained of his lack of talents, he made one last desperate attempt to escape: "O my Lord, send some other person!"

Do these protests sound familiar? We haven't invented any fresh excuses in all these thousands of years. Like Moses, when challenged to serve, we think first of ourselves and concentrate on our own weaknesses. We don't want to appear foolish, weak, or stupid. In our preoccupation with preserving our self-image, we fail to see that God has offered all of his resources and has promised to sustain those who accept his assignments.

Do you remember these?

"He gives power to the faint, and to him who

has no might he increases strength" (Isa. 40:29).

"*But you, take courage! Do not let your hands be weak, for your work shall be rewarded*" (2 Chron. 15:7).

How different the history of the people of Israel would have been if Moses had let fear dominate and had continued to refuse to let God use him!

Who's afraid? Paul was afraid and he freely admitted it. Writing to the church at Corinth he said, ". . . when I came to proclaim to you God's secret purpose, I did not come equipped with any brilliance of speech or intellect. You may as well know now that it was my secret determination to concentrate entirely on Jesus Christ himself and the fact of his death upon the cross. As a matter of fact, *in myself I was feeling far from strong. I was nervous and rather shaky*. What I said and preached had none of the attractiveness of the clever mind, but it was a demonstration of the power of the Spirit of God! Plainly God's purpose was that your faith should rest not upon man's cleverness but upon the power of God" (1 Cor. 2:1-5, Phillips version).

There is a measure of comfort in knowing that a man of Paul's stature had moments when he felt nervous! But he rose above it by concentrating on Jesus Christ. He recognized that if he had been clever or capable himself, it might have detracted from his message about Christ.

It may seem a far, far cry from the chairman of a circle meeting to Moses and Paul. But all three are servants of God, called out for a specific task. Each is dependent upon God, and only in recognizing this can natural human fears and nervousness be overcome. Paul put it well when he wrote, "Not that we are sufficient of ourselves to claim anything as coming from us; our sufficiency is from God" (Phil. 4:12).

Who's afraid? Not the person who like Paul says and believes, *"I can do* all things in him who strengthens me" (Phil. 4:13).

When They Leave Home

Where did you leave Daniel? In the lions' den? Perhaps that dramatic story of deliverance is about all you recall about this amazing young man from Sunday school days. If you are a mother of sons who will be leaving home to go into service or away to college (even if they are still only infants—perhaps *especially* if they are still babies, for then you will have time to give them the right foundation), it will be enlightening and encouraging for you to read again at least the first six chapters of the Old Testament book of Daniel. There you will see how Daniel got along in the world after his home ties were cut.

Daniel was drafted. In those days, as now, only the best were accepted for service, "youths without blemish, handsome and skillful in all wisdom, endowed with knowledge, understanding, learning, and competent to serve . . . and to teach" (Dan. 1:4).

These young servicemen were to have three years of basic training. During that time they would be taught "the letters and the language of the Chaldeans." They were subjected to new and heathen philosophies and to radically different ideas that conflicted with the simple faith which they had learned in their homes. Since they would have to face an examination at the end of their education, they were expected to learn all they could. Daniel and his three buddies were the top students in the group. They had applied themselves diligently to learning what was offered (in full academic freedom), but they were so solidly grounded in their faith that they were not shocked, shaken, or swayed by the tempting intellectualism to which they were exposed. They were able to resist. They studied *about* these ideologies, but they did not *believe* them.

Life in the service was vastly different from what they had known. As our boys get serial numbers which become even more important identifications than their names, these young men were given new names. This was a technique calculated to remove them even one step farther from home ties. When they were given rich food and wines, again Daniel resisted. He "resolved that he would not defile himself with the king's rich food, or with the wine which he drank," so he appealed to the officers for permission to change his diet. "God gave him favor and compassion in their sight," and they agreed to let him do so. When it was demonstrated that his health and strength improved, his resistance was recognized, respected, and it actually resulted in the regulations being changed for all.

Young people away from home and the solidarity of the family unit need to shore up their personal resolve in the counsel and encouragement of good friends who share their basic convictions. Daniel had found such friends in the service, and they sustained one another when the going was rough. As Daniel came more and more to the attention of the authorities, who recognized that he had great potential, he depended heavily upon his three buddies who had such rhythmic, tongue-twisting names: Shadrach, Meshach, and Abednego. Daniel talked over his problems with them, and they sought "the mercy of the God of heaven." They prayed together, and in their prayer fellowship all were strengthened.

Youth under pressure of majority opinion or social conformity so often fear that unless they shape themselves to the accepted standards they will suffer both in their social and their professional lives. Not so with Daniel. Even though he took a firm and independent stand for his convictions, his brilliance and capability were recognized, and he got one promotion after another. On his recommendation, his three friends were also given important government positions, and in their jobs they continued faithful to their God.

Naturally this eventually led to persecution. Shadrach, Meshach, and Abednego, who refused to worship the golden image of the king, were thrown into a fiery furnace that was heated to seven times its normal temperature. But they were protected and came out untouched. Even "the hair of their heads was not singed" and they didn't even smell of fire when they came out.

Daniel, who had become the chief of the wise

men, was the third ruler of the land, and about to become the royal prime minister of the whole kingdom, deliberately defied the law of the land in order to continue his personal prayer life. Then he was locked in with the lions but God closed their mouths. Righteousness was his sure defense, and purity was his armor. Man had carried out the sentence of human law but God had thwarted its fulfillment. Even in the face of apparently impossible odds, God is on the side of his own. When the state demands allegiance that belongs only to God, then the state stands under divine judgment.

Young people ought to know these things and have confidence in their faith in God. Faith can do much more than protect from danger and provide a way of escape from persecution.

With Daniel, faith in God was obviously a way of life. Even the king noticed it. When this young man was about to face the lions, the king unwittingly commended him for his faithfulness, "May your God, *whom you serve continually,* deliver you!" Again, when Daniel was in the den, the king asked anxiously, "Has your God, *whom you serve continually,* been able to deliver you from the lions?" Faith was no "on-again-off-again" thing with Daniel. He had a steadfast, unswerving loyalty to the God in whom he had put his trust.

Always and in every situation he found that God was dependable.

When your young men and women leave the shelter of home will they go armed with the kind of faith that can withstand the assault of contradictory philosophies and ideologies? Will they have the courage to stand firmly for moral principles? Will they deliberately seek out friends who will be mutually upbuilding? Will they remain on the side of righteousness in spite of consequences? Will they serve God continually, or only spasmodically when it seems convenient?

Daniel left home with that kind of faith, and Daniel prospered.

What Do You See?

Our art instructor was much wiser than we thought. Most of us in the night school class were frustrated and rebellious after six weeks of instruction in elementary drawing and sketching. He hadn't yet demonstrated how we should form an ear or a nose. He hadn't given us any help in guiding our wavering pencils. He just let us struggle along at each session, trying as best we could to reproduce on our drawing boards the various cubes, cylinders, vases, and drapery that he arranged on a table as models.

Gradually it dawned on us what he was trying to do. Over and over again he repeated, "Look at the model—really *look* at it and then draw what you see."

The trouble with us was that we were looking but not seeing. He was trying to teach us to observe the contours of each object, to become aware of the source of light and to notice the location of the shadows. Until we learned to use our eyes and really see what was before us we couldn't possibly begin to transfer a recognizable image to the paper.

Most of us don't use our eyes to full advantage. We see, but we do not always perceive.

When Jesus healed the man who was born blind, he opened his eyes so he could look around him for the first time. But there is an equally interesting miracle evident in his progressive awareness as he looked at Jesus.

He saw him first only as "a man called Jesus." He explained to his neighbors that this man had done a marvelous thing for him, something that had never been done before for one who was born blind. He saw his benefactor as a gentle, kind person who was worthy of honor and respect because of his skill and thoughtfulness.

This is the limit of the vision of many people: they look at Jesus and they see him as a man among men. They recognize him as a significant figure in history. They admire his many qualities. They acknowledge his deeds of mercy and his compassion for suffering humanity. And that is all they see.

When pressed for an explanation of how the healing could be called a good thing when Jesus obviously broke a Sabbath law to do it, the man was given further illumination, and his spiritual eyes were opened a little bit wider. "He is a prophet," the man declared, sensing that Jesus must have some special connection with God. This miracle must be a sign that Jesus was some-one set apart. "If this man were not from God he could do nothing," he concluded.

That Jesus somehow is in touch with God and the recipient of some special revelations is readily admitted by many who look at him and see him as a great spiritual teacher. They marvel at the depth of his philosophical reasoning and the wisdom of his simple logic. They admire his intellect. They look at him, but they do not see the source of his light.

The questioning, needling curiosity continued and grew in intensity. The man could only protest, "All I know is that though I was blind, now I see." It was enough for him. He could not be anything but loyal to one who had done so much for him. And as so often happens, loyalty to Jesus resulted in his rejection by his fellows. But as may also be expected, Jesus did not abandon him. He returned. The man looked at Jesus again, and his loyalty was rewarded with sharper spiritual vision. Suddenly he really saw Jesus. He knew then that human characterization was inadequate. He perceived that this was truly the Son of God.

"Lord," he said, "I believe," and he worshiped him.

What do you see in Jesus? A man? A teacher? Or the Lord?

What Is Your Frame of Mind?

Such a question wants to know what you think —what your mental attitude is. It also wants to know how you feel—what your emotional climate is.

Usually we consider the mind to be the source of our thoughts and the heart to be the center of our feelings, but actually they are so much intertwined that it is not easy to separate them or to know which determines the frame of mind.

Scripture many times uses the terms "heart" and "mind" interchangeably. For example, it speaks of thoughts coming from the heart: "Out of the heart come evil thoughts." And it speaks of the heart as having wisdom: "If your heart is wise, my heart too will be glad." The Bible uses the word "mind" in reference to the emotional attitudes of pride and anxiety: "Be not high-minded" in the King James version is translated "Do not become proud." In Luke 12:29 it says, ". . . do not be of anxious mind."

Reasoning, thinking, feeling, willing are all involved in frame of mind. This is the general "bent" or direction of our emotional and mental attitudes and it becomes the motivation of our behavior. These things cannot be strictly separated or rigidly categorized.

"Gird up your minds," wrote Peter, "be sober, set your hope fully upon the grace that is coming to you at the revelation of Jesus Christ" (1 Peter 1:13). To gird up our minds is to control what we think and how we feel. This requires exerting some real effort. Our natural inclination, unfortunately, is not toward what is pure and noble, but we can turn in the direction of what is good and determine to lift our thoughts and feelings to higher levels.

Scripture suggests that we ought to adapt our attitudes to those of Christ. "Let this mind be in you, which was also in Christ Jesus," means that we ought to take the long (eternal) view of things and to try to see them in the light of his kind of sacrificial love. This is the way Christ approached life and its many problems, and it is the example for us to follow.

One of the things we ought to do is to condition our thinking so we can get along with other people. When Scripture admonishes us to "Be of the same mind," it implies that we ought to strive to find common ground and a common outlook with others so that we can live at peace with our neighbors. Such a frame of mind would not be set in its own opinions; it would be flexible, considerate, conciliatory, forgiving, and tolerant.

Much of life is sordid and ugly. It bids for our attention, but Christians will deliberately lift their thoughts and affections above the things which degrade. "Set your mind on things that are above," it says in Col. 3:2. This means that we will not see only the smut and filth, but we will make a conscious effort to concentrate on better things. "Whatever is true, whatever is honorable, whatever is just, whatever is pure, whatever is lovely, whatever is gracious, if there is any excellence, if there is anything worthy of praise, think about these things" (Phil. 4:8). This could well be a guide to reading material, entertainment, and even conversation. The person who dwells continually on what is low and base will become low and base. One who thinks pure thoughts and gives his attention to what is holy and righteous will become a better person. "As he thinketh within himself so he is."

It takes real effort to exercise control over our hearts and minds, but many of the scriptural admonitions say that we must do this. "Take every thought captive to obey Christ," it says in 2 Cor. 10:5. Some of the effort must be our own, but, fortunately, there is help available to us.

Paul gave the Romans some distinct guidelines for their behavior as "living sacrifices" in response to God's great mercy and love toward them. He recognized, however—what we must also recognize—that to take the path of least resistance and follow the world's way is to fail miserably. "Don't let the world around you squeeze you into its own mold," he wrote, "but let God remold your minds from within" (Phillips).

It is not enough simply to make the supreme effort to change your own heart and mind. It is a matter of self-discipline *and* the power of the Holy Spirit. Mere reformation is not enough; there must also be regeneration. If we want to rid our hearts and minds of evil, the simple act of faith in Christ will cleanse, and then the living, indwelling Spirit will keep them clean.

The Holy Spirit will help us if we let him. He will change our hearts, minds, and attitudes so that we can live the Christian life as we should— but it is still up to us to choose a frame of mind that is turned in the right direction.

What is your frame of mind?

Beside Ourselves

"I'm absolutely beside myself!" the young mother exclaimed as she corralled her three children and guided them and a grocery cart through the check-out lane.

At best, grocery shopping is a chore, but it can

be a real ordeal when it includes keeping tab on three curious, lively youngsters in the labyrinth of temptation in a supermarket while trying to select a week's menu for the family. This frustrated woman had reached the ragged end of her patience when she used that curious but expressive phrase "beside myself" to describe her state.

The expression suggests a sort of shadowy other self standing beside one, pulling and tugging in all directions at once. The dictionary defines "beside oneself" as "out of one's wits or senses; crazy." The shopping mother was certainly not that badly off, but she was at a point of some kind of desperation and about ready to "throw in the towel" and give up.

In the Old Testament book of Job there is a description of how human beings would react if exposed to the full force of the power of God. "When he raises himself up the mighty are afraid; at the crashing they are *beside themselves*" (Job 41:25). Even the strongest men can be reduced to quivering terror when God shows his power in the elements, and such fear can literally drive people out of themselves.

The expression appears again in the New Testament. This time, strangely enough, the disciples used it in describing Jesus. "He is *beside himself*,"

they said, and the scribes agreed, "He is possessed
by Beelzebul." The incident is recorded in Mark
3. Jesus had cast out some demons, and the disciples, misunderstanding what he was doing,
jumped to the conclusion that he must be insane.
The people, fascinated by the sensational, pressed
in upon him. The disciples became frightened.
Believing that Jesus was mentally deranged, they
wanted to protect him from the mob. Jesus, always
patient with the blindness of the disciples, took
time right then to help them understand what he
was doing.

Paul was accused of being an offbeat eccentric.
Once he said that he was not afraid to be a "fool
for Christ's sake." In writing to the Corinthians he
tried to clarify this. He was not trying to draw
attention to himself, but he said his noncon-
formity was for the cause of God. "For if we are
beside ourselves, it is for God." Paul's motives
were neither selfish nor crazy. He was concerned
only with advancing the kingdom of God by whatever means seemed necessary. In all things, he
said, "the love of Christ controls."

The Prodigal Son, lured away from home by the
tantalizing glitter of the big, wide world, finally
reached the end of his rope. He had sunk so low
that he was scrounging around the pigpen, snatch-

ing husks away from the swine to hold off starvation. This proud young man had been reduced to nothing. He had nothing, and Scripture says, "No one gave him anything." At this low point certainly he was "beside himself," almost out of his mind with fear, anxiety, and humiliation. "But when *he came to himself* . . . ," it says in Luke 15:17, he knew he had hit the bottom. Then he remembered how well his father's servants lived. It didn't damage his pride a bit more to decide to go back and offer himself to his father as a hired hand.

The tensions and pressures of life sometimes come upon us so thick and fast that we feel "beside ourselves." If we have been hypnotized by sin, or terrified by overwhelming elements, or driven to despair, we may come to the point where we are ready to give up. Then if we remember God, chuck our pride, and turn to him, we will find a loving, patient Father willing and eager to help. Some people, like the disciples in their blindness, may think we have lost our senses if we "let go and let God take over." But when we "come to ourselves," the frustration, fear, hopelessness will vanish.

"I waited patiently for the Lord; he inclined to me and heard my cry. He drew me up from the desolate pit, out of the miry bog, and set my feet upon a rock, making my steps secure. He put a new song in my mouth" (Ps. 40:1-3).

Since all the resources of God are available to us, certainly we must be "beside ourselves" if we continue to compete with the pigs for a share of their husks!

Consecrated, Lord, to Thee

"Can any of you help on Saturday?"

The chairman looked hopefully around the circle.

Silence.

One woman scrounged through her purse looking for the tiny calendar she carried. Others just stared at the floor.

"If there are several of us, we can do the job in a couple of hours," the chairman continued.

Silence.

"I'll be there, of course," the chairman said, "but I could really use just a little help."

One woman spoke up timidly. "Well, maybe I can come for a little while anyway." She looked frightened as though somehow she had betrayed the rest of the group by volunteering.

Another ventured, "I don't have time to help, but I'll contribute some money."

Here was a thought. Suddenly there was a flurry of apologies for inability to serve counterbalanced by almost eager offers of money for the project. The treasurer hastily made note of the promises for financial support.

The chairman had only one name and her own on the list of workers, but there seemed no point in pressing the issue any further. She announced the closing hymn and the women sang with gusto:

> *Take my life, and let it be*
> *Consecrated, Lord, to thee;*
>
> *Take my hands, and let them move*
> *At the impulse of thy love.*

It always seems much easier to give of what we have than to give of what we *are* for the service of the Lord. Perhaps this is because when we give a gift of money we are through and can forget it. When we give of our time and energy we become personally involved, and getting involved is the thing we seem to fear most of all.

A revised version of Frances Havergal's hymn of dedication suggests itself. It seems more appropriate to the situation and perhaps more honest than the original:

> *Take my wealth and let it be*
> *Consecrated 'stead of me—*
> *Take my dollars and my cents*
> *For my sloth to recompense.*
>
> *I will give—and generously,*
> *Only, please, don't bother me!*
> *Cash should always be resolved—*
> *But I don't want to get involved!*

Pie in the Sky

There was cherry pie for dessert on the jetliner that was taking me across country for a speaking engagement. Enjoying the last forkful as I idly watched fluffy white clouds below the plane, I remembered an old expression that cynical scoffers used to apply to Christians. They said, "The Christians are just waiting for 'pie in the sky by and by.'" Pie in the sky was exactly what I was having and enjoying every morsel!

The essence of Christian hope is, of course, a patient waiting for the fulfillment of our salvation in the future when we shall see Jesus face to face. We believe and depend on such promises as 2 Cor. 4:14, "We know for certain that he who raised the Lord Jesus from death shall also by him raise us. We shall all stand together before him" (Phillips version).

And we do look for "pie in the sky," or some type of heavenly reward. Paul put it this way, "The outward man does indeed suffer wear and tear, but every day the inward man receives fresh strength. These little troubles (which are really so transitory) are winning for us a permanent, glorious and solid reward out of all proportion to our pain. For we are looking all the time not at the visible things but at the invisible. The visible things are transitory: it is the invisible things that are really permanent" (2 Cor. 4:16-18 Phillips).

We often use the word "hope" casually and loosely so that it conveys little more than wishful thinking. We say, "I hope it stops raining." "I hope everything turns out OK." When we use the word in regard to our expectation for the successful outcome of a business deal it is an expression only of the anticipation of temporal profit.

Christian hope is much more than wishful thinking or the prospect of reward. It is a firm expectation based on the fundamental fact of the resurrection of Christ. "In his great mercy we men have been born again into a life full of hope, through Christ's rising again from the dead! You can now hope for a perfect inheritance beyond the reach of change and decay, 'reserved' in heaven for you. And in the meantime you are guarded by the power of God operating through your faith, till you enter fully into the salvation which is all ready for the dénouement of the last day" (1 Peter 1:3-5 Phillips).

Christian hope reaches up and holds on to the things that are not seen but which are assured to us through the promise of the resurrection of Christ. Hope, thus, is dependent upon faith—for we hope for that in which we believe.

It is a frightful thing to be devoid of any kind of hope. When everything else collapses, it is still possible to pick up the pieces of a seemingly impossible situation and make a fresh beginning if one has just a glimmer of hope. When hope too is gone, there truly is complete defeat. Hope sees light in darkness. Hope clings to its promise of the future and borrows on that security for confidence today.

Charles Allen, in his book *All Things Are Possible Through Prayer* (Fleming H. Revell), wrote that "the real profanity of man is not some swear words he may say. These words are more stupid than sinful. The most profane word we can use is the word 'hopeless' because it is slamming the door in the face of God to consider that any situation or any person is hopeless."

To call a situation or a person "hopeless" is to assume that it or he is beyond the reach of God's redemption.

Hope is the framework of our purpose. It becomes a kind of goal toward which we direct our finest efforts. If our hope is in Christ and we expect, on the basis of his righteousness, to achieve a place in the kingdom of heaven, then we will direct our lives toward that future. It is natural to reach and stretch toward that for which we hope. And it is this tendency which makes false hopes so dangerous.

If all we can answer is, "I hope so," to a question about our right relationship with Christ, then we need to do something quickly. Merely to hope that God is in his heaven and therefore everything is going to be right with the world and your own eternal soul is to build on a pretty uncertain foundation.

We need to know—and we *can* know, for assurance is one of the gifts that the Holy Spirit transmits through the Word: "For all those words which were written long ago are meant to teach us today; that when we read in the scriptures of the endurance of men and of all the help that God gave them in those days, we may be encouraged to go on hoping in our own time. . . . May the God of hope fill you with joy and peace in your faith, that by the power of the Holy Spirit, your whole life and outlook may be radiant with hope" (Rom. 15:4, 13 Phillips).

Christian hope is not a vague guess. It is sure knowledge of, and trust in, Christ and his resurrection. With this kind of confidence we can afford to be patient, because we know that God is in control. We can afford to endure, because we know that right will ultimately triumph. We need have no fear of death, because death for the Christian becomes only a transition into the presence of God where that for which we have hoped will at last be realized.

Ridicule won't disturb a Christian whose "hope is built on nothing less than Jesus' blood and righteousness." He will look forward with eager anticipation to "pie in the sky by and by" and all the other glorious things he has been promised.

How Much Are We Worth?

Thirty-five years ago a scientist made news when he announced that the chemicals in the human body could be purchased for only 98 cents. Now, with the increased cost of living, our chemical value, like everything else, has soared to an astounding new high. Now we are worth a whopping $800, according to an executive of a large chemical company.

At various times in the world's history, life has been notoriously cheap. In pagan Rome, for instance, the best strong young men were pitted against starved wild animals just to provide entertainment in the Coliseum. In many heathen cultures, girl babies, considered worthless, were killed without qualms. Carelessness and disease have wiped out people by the millions in many underdeveloped countries. The value placed on human life seems to be in direct proportion to the degree of civilization (though our highway toll gives reason to wonder how high a price we put on human life).

Psychologically it is important to know that we have some worth as persons. Our human dignity depends on it. We need to feel that we are acceptable and that we are making some useful contribution to society.

When troubles pile up and everything seems to go wrong, our first impulse is to question our own worth. In our despair we see ourselves as useless.

When Job hit rock bottom in his troubles, he questioned the value of man in the total scheme of things. He said, "Man that is born of woman is of few days, and full of trouble. He comes forth like a flower, and withers; he flees like a shadow, and continues not."

Unfortunately, poor Job didn't get too much encouragement from the friends who came to comfort him. One of them said, "Can a man be profitable to God? Is it any pleasure to the Almighty if you are righteous, or is it gain to him if you make your ways blameless?" Another of his friends, who had an even dimmer view, compared man to a maggot or a worm.

When we see our own sinfulness and are overwhelmed by it, our tendency is to grovel in our unworthiness. Sometimes we even take a perverse kind of pride in our very humility! One of the old prayer hymns that attempts to set a proper tone of humility has these words, "though dust and ashes in thy sight . . . ." The Psalmist in one of his moments of self-disgust cried out, "But I am a worm and no man . . . ." And another time the Psalmist expressed amazement that God even bothers with man, "What is man that thou dost regard him?" It seems hard to believe we have not put ourselves beyond the reach of God's concern.

At the other extreme, however, when we feel on top of the world and things go well, there is the terrible temptation to price ourselves too high and to overevaluate our worth. Then it is that "The pride of your heart has deceived you" and "A man's pride will bring him low." The Phillips version of Gal. 6:3 puts it this way, "If a man thinks he is somebody, he is deceiving himself, for that very thought proves he is nobody."

How much are we worth? Actually nothing. We aren't even alive: *"you were dead* through trespasses and sins." But God, who is rich in mercy, out of his great love has made us alive together with Christ. "For by grace you have been saved through faith; and this is not your own doing, it is a *gift of God."* Accepting this in faith, we are given royal status: "For in Christ Jesus you are all *sons* of God through faith."

In estimating our own worth, we ought never

to forget that we are children of God with access to all the resources of his kingdom. We should neither grovel in self-abasement that dishonors our royal heritage, nor should we strut in self-righteous pride that fails to acknowledge the gifts of God. "Don't cherish exaggerated ideas of yourself or your importance, but try to have a sane estimate of your capabilities by the light of the faith that God has given to you all" (Rom. 12:3-4 Phillips).

"The fact is that what we are we owe to the hand of God upon us."

Accepting ourselves, then, and acknowledging God's gifts, we can use them in full confidence that he will bless the results. "Not that we are sufficient of ourselves to claim anything as coming from us; our sufficiency is from God."

What are we worth to God? We are personally known and valued by him as Isaiah 43 indicates: "Fear not, for I have redeemed you; I have called you by name, you are mine . . . you are precious in my eyes, and honored, and I love you."

What is man? A flower that withers? A worm? Dust and ashes? No, we are individually loved and worth so much to God that he came down to die for us!

"... *Its Inhabitants Are Like Grasshoppers* ..."

An elderly lady making her first plane trip was almost numb with fright. When she had fastened her seat belt, she shut her eyes and waited rigidly for the worst to happen. The huge motors roared into throbbing life and the plane vibrated furiously. At last the little lady had courage enough to open her eyes and peer down from the window. Then she turned to her seatmate, "Isn't it amazing," she said, "those people down there look just like grasshoppers!"

The gentleman beside her glanced up from his magazine and replied, "They are grasshoppers—we haven't taken off yet!"

When Isaiah wrote about the sovereignty and the mightiness of God, he spoke of him as one "who sits above the circle of the earth, and its inhabitants are like grasshoppers" (Isa. 40:22).

It is impossible to consider the bigness and the majesty of God without at the same time being aware of the smallness of man by comparison.

It was just such a revelation that caused the

Psalmist to cry out, "O Lord, our Lord, how majestic is thy name in all the earth! . . . When I look at thy heavens, the work of thy fingers, the moon and the stars which thou hast established; what is man that thou art mindful of him, and the son of man that thou dost care for him?" (Ps. 8:1, 3, 4).

And Job, who probably knew this Psalm, when he was sorely tried and tested by God, cried out, "What is man, that thou dost make so much of him, and that thou dost set thy mind upon him, dost visit him every morning, and test him every moment?" (Job 7:17-18).

In contrast to God, man is not much. But on the other hand, man does not always see God in his true proportions either.

J. B. Phillips, British writer and lecturer, once asked a group of students, "Does God know about radar?" The reply was a resounding, "No." But then a ripple of laughter ran through the audience as they realized the absurdity of their answer.

This spontaneous reply revealed that subconsciously these students conceive of God as an elderly gentleman of another era who just hasn't kept pace with scientific progress. God created us in his image, but too often we think of him as a replica of ourselves with the same human limitations we have.

The Christian woman who would determine her own stature and her place in the world needs first to see how big and how able and how dependable is the God in whom she has put her confidence.

Isaiah describes him as "The everlasting God, the Creator of the ends of the earth. He does not faint or grow weary, his understanding is unsearchable." Such a God ought to be capable of controlling all that he has created. But how can so great a God care about each individual "grasshopper" who inhabits the earth that he has made? Can the God who made the vast universe, where the sun we see is only one of a hundred billion suns, be concerned about how each of us insignificant beings lives his little life?

God not only understands radar and the atom and innumerable other things which scientific knowledge has uncovered, but he made them in the first place, and he has kept many of his miracles in reserve for our discovery and use from time to time in the future.

More important than his unsearchable understanding of the cosmic forces, however, is his understanding of the heart of each human soul. He knows the limits of our strength and endurance and "he gives power to the faint, and to him who has no might he increases strength." Although Isaiah saw us as grasshoppers, he also added that "those who wait for the Lord shall mount up with wings like eagles . . . run and not be weary . . . walk and not faint."

God considers all of us to be his well beloved children, and he wants all of us to come to a knowledge of his salvation. "In this the love of God was made manifest among us, that God sent his only Son into the world so that we might live through him" (1 John 4:9).

It is unlikely that God would have given his only Son to die for grasshoppers!

Clean-up Job

We had not heard of "instant mixes" in those days, but we knew that if we mixed some of the dirt at the edge of the garden with a little water from the rain barrel, it was perfect for mud pies. My playmate and I spent long hours mixing batter and forming pies in Mason jar covers which we would set in the sun to bake. In the process, of course, we usually got pretty dirty.

One day my playmate had a new idea for using her left-over dough. She washed her hands in it!

She plunged her hands deep into the mud, pulled them out, and then plunged them in again. It was great fun! So I put my hands in, too, and laved the mud generously up both arms to the elbow. Laughing hilariously, my friend imitated this new twist of the game. Then we decided to plaster some of the mud on our faces. Looking at each other and realizing how different we looked we wondered if our mothers would even recognize us. So we went to my house and rang the front doorbell.

We should have known better—but four-year-olds don't usually think through an impulse to its consequences!

There was no doubt about it—my mother knew who we were. Under all the mud she recognized me as her child, but she wouldn't let us come into the house. In that moment she didn't disown me, but she was obviously angry about my filthy condition. She didn't appreciate our handiwork—she didn't even think it was funny. She just took us around to the back yard. There she used the garden hose to rinse off the worst of the dirt before she sent my little friend home and took me into the house for more thorough cleansing, a fresh starched dress—and a lecture!

When thinking of God and our relationship to him, I often remember that day from childhood.

Washing and cleansing are necessary and important to our spiritual lives too. We become God's own children through the deep cleansing of the washing of regeneration in Baptism. But as we live day by day we get dirty again and need repeated clean-up jobs.

Sometimes we have such a good time we don't realize that we are sinning and that our souls are getting as soiled as though we were deliberately smearing them with mud. Like foolish children, we don't see beyond the moment to its results. In our preoccupation with what we are doing, we forget who we are—that we are the children of a perfectly holy and clean God who abhors sin. And we forget that by willful disobedience we get dirty, not only on the outside, but we also become internally defiled.

Yet even under all the filth and dirt with which sin disguises us, God recognizes us as his beloved children. Like a parent, he is distressed by our behavior, for he hates sin and the effect it has upon us. In our unclean state we cannot have our proper parent-child relationship but we must first be made clean, for "nothing unclean shall enter it" (the city of God).

He loves his children, even when they are unclean sinners, "for God has not called us for uncleanness, but in holiness" (1 Thess. 4:7), therefore he has provided for our cleansing so that we may be made fit to come into his holy presence. "The blood of Jesus his Son cleanses us from all sin" (1 John 1:7). And this cleansing takes care of not only the external dirt but also the internal defilement from a rebellious and evil spirit. The perfect obedience of Jesus makes such complete cleansing possible because his righteousness is transferred to our account. He was pure not only in his deeds but in his attitude and spirit, too. This is God's great gift of grace—if we repent and believe in Jesus, all he is and all that he has becomes ours.

Some people are like small boys who protest, "Why wash my hands—they'll only get dirty again!" These people have no desire to change their condition; they refuse even to admit that they are unclean, and stoutly resist any attempt to clean them up.

Some people have been baptized and expect it to last them a lifetime. They don't realize that they are in need of daily cleansing since contact with the world is bound to make them unclean—at least in spots! This is as ridiculous as to claim that since you once had a bath you should always stay clean!

Sometimes we know how dirty we are. We see ourselves exactly the way we are when we look into the mirror of the Word of God. Then, like the Psalmist, we cry out for cleansing. "Wash me thoroughly from my iniquity and cleanse me from my sin!" (Ps. 51:2).

Paul, writing to Titus, mentioned how much we are like foolish children who play in the mud, heedless of the consequences.

"For we ourselves were once foolish, disobedient, led astray, slaves to various passions and pleasures, passing our days in malice and envy, hated by men and hating one another; but when the goodness and loving kindness of God our Savior appeared, he saved us, not because of deeds done by us in righteousness, but in virtue of his own mercy, by the washing of regeneration and renewal in the Holy Spirit, which he poured out upon us richly through Jesus Christ our Savior, so that we might be justified by his grace and become heirs in hope of eternal life" (Titus 3:3-7).

We keep getting dirty, for we continue to sin, but how wonderful it is to have a Father God who also will continue to clean us up!

Someone Else's Shoes

I got caught in the rain one day and my shoes were completely soaked. Rather than pad around the office in my stockings, I accepted the offer of one of the girls to wear an extra pair that she had.

The size was perfect. They were old, soft shoes that should have been quite comfortable. Almost immediately, however, I discovered something I hadn't known before. My ankles tend to lean toward each other when I walk! Apparently my generous friend has ankles that incline in the other direction. She had worn the shoes long enough so that they were shaped to her pattern of walking. This made them all wrong for me.

I realized from this that while we might both purchase the same size, after we had worn them, our shoes would cease to be alike. They would soon take on a new shape that would reflect our own particular manner of walking.

The fact that my ankles happen to turn in doesn't make me any better than she is. And certainly my friend isn't superior to me because she wears her heels down at another slant. Like our separate personalities, our shoes are personal and not really interchangeable.

It reminded me of the old Indian saying that goes something like this, "You must not criticize another person until you have walked a mile in his moccasins."

Obviously I had no right to criticize my benefactor, for I couldn't possibly have walked a mile in her shoes! But as I hobbled around the office, the moral of the old proverb became very clear.

People are individuals. We are all different, and we are entitled to be different. We ought, then, to learn to be tolerant of one another and to develop some understanding of the qualities that make us unique. If we could "walk in their moccasins," that is, if we could enter fully into their experience so that we would know what makes them the way they are, we might see things from their point of view.

I expect the wise Indian who coined the expression wasn't thinking about how badly the neighbor's moccasins might fit. Rather, I think he was suggesting that we ought to make the effort to understand what factors have cooperated to shape his attitudes and his personality, so we can accept him as he is.

It isn't easy to project yourself into another's life and experience to the extent that you feel what he feels, suffers as he suffers, or are happy as he is happy. It is much easier to stand in judgment and to criticize and condemn him on the basis of how things look from where we see it. What we see may be very different from the way things look from his vantage point. Blind, unreasoning criticism that doesn't allow for another side to the question doesn't usually help. More likely it builds a wall of resentment almost impossible to surmount.

Paul made quite a point of the necessity of tolerant understanding. He wrote to the Ephesians, "Accept life with humility and patience, *making allowances for each other* because you love each other. Be kind to each other, *be understanding.* Be as ready to forgive others as God for Christ's sake has forgiven you . . . *try to fit in with each other,* just because you all recognize that God is the supreme power over all." To the Colossians he wrote, "Accept life *and be most patient and tolerant with one another* . . . ." To the Philippians he wrote, "Do nothing from selfishness or conceit, but *in humility count others better than yourselves.*" And to the Romans he wrote, "We who are strong ought to bear with the failings of the weak, and not to please ourselves; *let each of us please his neighbor for his good, to edify him*" (Phillips version).

This is "walking a mile in his moccasins" according to the Scriptures. It may be uncomfortable, and we may limp badly when we do it, but it may help build a bridge of love to our neighbor. It may help us understand what makes him the way he is. It may give us tolerance and the grace to forgive. It may show us a practical way to help him in his need.

What Happened to Time?

Where did it go? What happened to the year just past? It seems such a short time since last Easter when we rejoiced in the reassurance that his dramatic resurrection proved Jesus to be the Son of God as he had claimed.

What happened to that whole year? Isn't it disturbing to look back and to be unable to point to any significant accomplishments and to see very little evidence of any increase in your love and concern for others?

Now a whole year has passed since you rejoiced in the sure and firm knowledge that Jesus died for your sins. Did the realization of such love leave you a little awe-stricken and at least temporarily determined to respond? Or were you satisfied to be a passive recipient of the tremendous grace of God and unmoved by any desire to respond?

What happened to that bundle of time that came to you moment by moment during the past year? Did it slip away as it came—moment by moment—without your grasping and using any of it for any really good purpose?

Time has to be used as it comes. It can't be used while it is still in the future and it is too late to use after it becomes the past. It has to be used in the "now," in the present moment. But that present moment is so fleeting that before you realize it, it has passed from the future through the present and into the past. Then it is lost and gone forever. And so are the opportunities you might have acted upon in that little segment of time between the future and the past.

How did you miss it?

Perhaps you were preoccupied with other missed opportunities of other years. Perhaps you were so burdened with the guilt of past misdeeds and omissions that you never quite caught up to the "now" with its fresh chance to do something worth while.

Perhaps you were so troubled and anxious

about the future and its uncertainties that you couldn't concentrate your attention on creative ways to make use of the present moment. Either guilt about the past or fear of the future can paralyze us for effective use of the present and that is the only time we have in which to respond to the love of God by serving God and our fellow-men.

How tragic it is to miss the present moment! How unproductive it is to dwell on the past and its mistakes! How futile to cringe in fear of the future! It is precisely because of our past sins that Christ died on the cross. If we confess our sins in prayer to God and accept his forgiveness, we can forget the past! Then we are free!

Nor do we need to waste a single moment of the precious "now" stewing about what is to be. Certainly the assurance that Jesus was actually the divine Son of God who endured the humiliation of becoming a man and dying a shameful death ought to convince us that God truly does care what happens to us. We should, of course, view the future sanely and plan for our needs sensibly, but we do not need to fret or worry about it. We can trust God to provide. We can trust him to take care of whatever eventualities may come. If we walk each day in his protective custody, simply trusting him to take care of us, we will be safe. This is another assurance the cross gives us: that he knows what the future holds even though it seems dim and uncertain to us, and he cares for us personally.

When God penetrated the wall of time and entered into the stream of human history in the person of Jesus Christ, he freed us from the guilty clutch of the past and from a fearful anticipation of the future. We are thus released to devote ourselves to the present moment, the only time we have in which to do his will.

What happens to time? It is here, and it is gone. Actually time has significance to us only while we are earthbound. If we use the present moment with a view to eternal values, when we reach the next milestone, such as another Easter, we can glance back and see progress toward the spiritual maturity which is the goal of every believer.

Riches

On her 80th birthday, an elderly friend evaluated her years in these words: "Life has been full of riches—rich in sorrow and rich in joy."

Life for her hadn't been all trouble and misery, although she had more than her share; nor had it been all pleasant and joyous, although she had experienced many high points of real jubilation. But rather, life for her had been a blending of sorrow and joy. After 80 years she gratefully called the result "rich."

To understand this attitude, one should understand the real character of joy.

Joy is not evanescent, so that it appears and disappears like a vapor. It is not a shot in the arm that temporarily anesthetizes the hurts and buoys up drooping spirits only to wear off when the going gets rough. Joy doesn't depend on circumstances, luck, fortunate developments, and outward success. It doesn't ebb and flow with feelings as a fickle, capricious emotion.

Joy is of the soul. It is an abiding, constant, sustaining peace. It is serene assurance of the goodness of God. It cannot be shaken by the vicissitudes of life.

Joy is actually the spirit of Christ firmly established in the human heart. It is the "Unspeakable gift" that came into the world when Jesus was born in the Bethlehem manger.

Mary knew this joy and it sustained her so that her confidence in him never faltered. Joy first came into her heart at the annunciation and it remained. When she shared her secret with her cousin who was also expecting a child, Elizabeth said that the unborn John "leaped for joy" within her womb.

The shepherds heard the message and received the gift even before they saw the child. When the angel said to them, "I bring you good news of a great joy," they believed, and immediately the gift of joy was theirs.

When the wise men saw the star which was to lead them to the Christ Child, "they rejoiced exceedingly with great joy." Even before they had a chance to present the riches they had brought as gifts for the Infant, they became the beneficiaries of the greater riches of God's gift of joy.

Joy is the gift of God to all who believe. When it is possessed wholeheartedly, nothing can shake it. Troubles will come in life, and there will be times of illness, persecution, and distress, but the joy will remain—warm, glowing, comforting and reassuring.

Joy was Christ's first gift, and it was one of his last. On the night before his Passion he said several things about joy: "These things I have spoken to you, that my joy may be in you, and that your joy may be full." He warned, "You will be sorrowful, but your sorrow will turn into joy." He told us how to keep joy at peak capacity: "Hitherto you have asked nothing in my name; ask, and you will receive, that your joy may be full."

Joy to the world, the Lord is come! Is this not the greatest of all possible riches?

From Manger to Cross

In one of the Advent hymns we sing, "*O how shall I receive thee?*" The end of the first stanza suggests humble service as one way: "*To do in spirit lowly all that may please thee best.*"

Mary received the announcement of her role as the mother of Jesus in that spirit. In exultation she burst forth in a song of praise for the magnificence of God, and in her impromptu expression of joy she made only brief reference to her own part in the tremendous mystery, marveling that God had "regarded the low estate of his hand-maiden."

Mary didn't understand, but she trusted. She didn't consider herself worthy of the honor, but she accepted her destiny with complete confidence in God. Her attention was fixed so unwaveringly upon the glory of God that she was scarcely aware of her own part in the event. Her Magnificat thus became a model of true worship —humbly selfless and focused upon God.

A distinctive feature of the Christian religion which sets it apart from all other religions and ethical systems is its condemnation of pride and its insistence upon humility. Pride, according to the Scriptures, is the root and essence of sin. It is attributing to self the honor and glory which belong to God. Humility, on the other hand, is a virtue that switches the direction from self to God.

It is not very popular to be humble these days. The term has been confused with spinelessness and weakness. Since we admire virility and respect self-assertiveness and aggressiveness, humility seems an undesirable trait. Today it is quite common for people to "blow their own horns" and to push themselves forward whenever they get a chance. In the present era of materialism, personal worth is determined by possessions, position, and power. Therefore, whatever it takes to achieve these goals is encouraged. It is not surprising, then, that humility has become outmoded. In a self-centered world it seems almost

ridiculous to be humble. It may even be dangerous, for the humble person might be trampled under foot by the proud who are in headlong pursuit
of their own desires.

Even in his day the teachings of Jesus seemed
to be upside down and out of harmony with a
common sense approach to life.

One of the first things he said in the Sermon
on the Mount (which was full of seeming con-
tradictions to accepted beliefs) was, "How happy
are the humble-minded, for the kingdom of
Heaven is theirs!" To the Pharisees he said, "For
everyone who makes himself important will become insignificant, while the man who makes himself insignificant will find himself important."

He said, "If any wanted to be successful in their
ministry they should adopt the humility of little
children and refuse all honors and positions of
privilege that would be offered to them." He told
them, "He who loses his life for my sake will find
it."

Always Jesus asked that they should forget their
own desires and not think of themselves. They
should offer their very lives for others, if necessary. His words were incomprehensible to those
who looked for personal advantage. They are as
incomprehensible to us today if we are self-

centered. Even more by his life and his deeds than by his strange words Jesus encouraged the virtue of Christian humility.

A manger stands at the beginning of the earthly life of the immortal Son of God and a cross at the end. Both the manger and the cross are symbols of the humility which characterized his entire ministry.

At the season of Advent, when we contemplate how we shall receive him, remember how Mary received the promise. Remember the manger where God emptied himself of all his glory to take the form of an infant. See the shadow of a cross cast over the humble manger

Who can be proud in the face of these evidences of God humbling himself?

How shall we receive him? In deep humility and gratitude for God's great Gift that has put heaven within our grasp.

Grains of Salt

When someone says, "You have to take her with a grain of salt," we usually translate the common metaphor to mean: this person is different, maybe even a little odd, but if we read the best meaning into what she says and put the best construction on what she does, she isn't too hard to take.

If her natural qualities are not seasoned with understanding and patience, this person is easily misunderstood. She may be very irritating to have around because of her strange ways and unorthodox ideas, but taken with a grain of tolerance she can fit into most situations.

Jesus, in the Sermon on the Mount, called Christians the "salt of the earth." Salt is a mineral that has special qualities for preserving, purifying, and giving pungent flavor to foods. When describing people, it must mean that they have the ability to perform these valuable functions in society: preserving peace and harmony, purifying attitudes and atmosphere, adding spice and zest to living, and permeating all they meet with their Christian love.

There are both types—those who are salt and those who have to be taken with a grain of salt. There are those who are tolerant and those who have to be tolerated.

The best of us need a good deal of understanding, for we all have some strange ways and irritating qualities of personality. But all of us have the potential of being salt.

Paul was much concerned about Christians being loving, patient, understanding, and tolerant. If we are, he said, we will inevitably be at peace with one another. In writing to the Ephesians, he said, ". . . make allowances for one another because you love one another . . . fit in with one another, because of your common reverence for Christ."

To the Philippians he wrote, ". . . live together in harmony, live together in love, as though you had only one mind and one spirit between you . . . none of you should think only of his own affairs, but each should learn to see things from other people's point of view."

To the Colossians he spoke again of the need for Christians to make concessions for the faults and weaknesses of others when he says, ". . . accept life, and be most patient and tolerant with one another."

When Jesus called Christians the salt of the earth he warned that some of them lose their quality of saltiness and when they do, they have become useless. He said ". . . if salt has lost its taste, how shall its saltness be restored? It is no longer good for anything except to be thrown out and trodden under foot by men."

Which are you? Are you one of the salty ones

who puts himself in the other person's place and tries to see it from his point of view with sympathetic and patient understanding? Are you one who needs to be taken with a grain of salt, blundering along, slightly out of step with everyone else, needing a great deal of forgiveness and understanding? Or are you the third type of which Jesus warned?

Did You Make It From Scratch?

Whenever someone with a mouthful of my fresh-baked cake asks, "Did you use a mix or make it from scratch?" some of my pride of accomplishment disappears when I must confess that I have taken the easy way out of cake baking by using a prepared mix.

Perhaps Grandmother ground her own flour. She may have helped plant and harvest the wheat from which it was ground. She churned the butter and possibly helped milk the cows that produced the cream. She cared for the chickens that laid the eggs. She stoked the big kitchen range and may also have chopped the wood for it.

I wonder if she, too, felt a pang of guilt when she took the easy way and purchased smooth, white, refined flour at the local store.

Making a cake is not as simple as it seems, even today. Not that it is hard to add a fresh egg and a cup of water. I mean that involved in that cake is a complex modern way of life.

Into this luscious, tender cake which I have made "from a box" has gone the research and study of skilled technicians in test kitchens where long years of experimentation have developed the right formula to make this miracle possible.

There is an intricate electrical system that cools my eggs and spins the beaters of my mixer. There are pumps, filtration plants, storage tanks, and a city-wide network of pipes that bring the cup of water to my kitchen. There is an automatically controlled heat regulator and a buzzer on my oven to remind me to remove it at just the right moment.

I can easily justify my easy life as far as the kitchen duty is concerned, for Grandmother never got much beyond her kitchen. She was not involved in civic affairs, nor did she put in an eight-hour day in the office. Demands on her time were neither so urgent nor from so many sources as those which I must try to satisfy.

Grandmother would be as helpless in my stainless steel and porcelain kitchen as I would have been trying to subdue her big black range with which she did battle daily. My "pressure" cooker would scare her to death, but then, I wouldn't know the first thing about churning butter!

I don't think either of us would want to trade places, however!

There is no doubt about it, our grandmothers lived in an entirely different world from the standpoint of family economy. In some ways we are poles apart. But in another sense, we have much in common.

With all our automation, world-wide contacts and interests, we women are as much the daughters of Eve as Grandmother was. Basically women have not changed much.

We have the same hungers, needs, and problems that were the lot of the first woman in the world. We want to love and be loved. We want social recognition and we need self-realization. We are instinctively creative. We are eager for wisdom, and, like Eve, in seeking it, we could easily be tempted to forsake our place in paradise.

Women in every age have been subject to all

manner of human weakness, for as the heirs of Eve, we have a natural tendency to sin.

Yet, women also have a deep capacity for love. Their native talents are turned easily into channels of beauty and charm. They can be leaders, or they can submerge themselves in the lives and aspirations of husband and children. In unselfish concern for the welfare of their families they can be living examples of the meaning of understanding and forgiveness.

Women haven't changed much—it is only externals which are different. We may occupy a different role in the family and community today than we would have a couple of generations ago, many different things may be expected of us, but our basic natures and qualities of womanliness are the same.

Life for women is both simple and complex, but our big problem is not whether we bake a cake from "scratch" or use a mix, our big problem is still within ourselves.

If we can find the place where the Lord wants us to serve him and our fellowmen; if we trust him and use our natural endowments to the best advantage, the sphere of our lives will be better because we are here, moving ahead with each advance of the science of living. For we must give our best where it is needed most. Today's mechanization, which brings so many of the good things, should not imprint itself on our spirits, but should be used to enrich the warm tenderness and love of which we, as women, are capable.

Be proud and grateful that you are a woman endowed as God has seen fit, and never, never feel guilty for keeping step with progress, if you are spiritually grounded in the unchanging Word of God—the timeless answer to every woman's deepest need in every age!

Thanks and Giving

The fruit-filled cornucopia, the plump, succulent turkey, and the other trappings of feasting are readily recognized symbols of that fall festival of Thanksgiving which even our country recognizes by Presidential Proclamation.

It is little more than pagan to gather the fruits of the field, utter a perfunctory word of thanks, stuff ourselves to a state of semi-consciousness, and stretch out comfortably before the TV to watch the Big Ten play football. Yet this is the way we observe Thanksgiving—quite self-indulgently!

Real thanks is expressed in giving not gorging. The more we have been blessed the more we can give. The more we give, the more thanksgiving there will be to God on our behalf. Thanks and giving just can't be separated if God is acknowledged as the giver of all good gifts. Nor is there true thanksgiving when there is only thanks and no giving.

Writing to the people of Corinth (2 Cor. 9:7-15), Paul put it this way: "The more you are enriched by God, the more scope will there be for generous giving, and your gifts, administered through us, will mean that many will thank God. For your giving does not end in meeting the wants of your fellow Christians. It also results in an overflowing tide of thanksgiving to God. Moreover, your very giving proves the reality of your faith, and that means that men thank God that you practice the gospel that you profess to believe in, as well as for the actual gifts you make to them and to others. And yet further, men will pray for you and feel drawn to you because you have obviously re-

ceived a generous measure of the grace of God"
(Phillips).

Do you secretly fear that you may give too
much? Are you concerned about your own "old
age" and its needs when you are touched by the
urge of generosity? Then think of this assurance
from the Word of God:

"After all, God can give you everything that you
need, so that you may always have sufficient both
for yourselves and for giving away to other people."

There is no cause for alarm—we won't cut ourselves short. God's promise is that the more we
share, the more we will get. Trust him to keep
that promise too.

The spiritual wealth we possess is not always
tangible. It is not easy to see forgiveness that has
restored us to sonship with Jesus. The comfort and
the assurance of protection and guidance and
strength that are in every part of the Word of God
are riches beyond measuring. When we recognize
them as such, we will be moved to "thank God
for his unspeakable gift" and constrained to give
expression to our thanks through giving. In this
sharing of both material and spiritual gifts with
which we have been blessed, there will be a ver-
itable "overflowing tide of thanksgiving to God."

Pass Time or Kill Time

I have just learned to knit and already I'm addicted!

This morning I came to work with red, bleary eyes and a headache—just because I couldn't quit knitting at a sensible hour last night and didn't get enough sleep. But what a fascinating hobby!

I had observed friends who are "knit-wits" (by that term I mean those who are smart enough to understand the mysteriously coded knitting instructions). They talk, laugh, even watch television and never miss a stitch. Waiting my turn with the dentist recently I fidgeted restlessly while the lady next to me sat calmly knitting. She seemed so relaxed, almost tranquilized by the rhythmic clicking of her needles. Too long I have stood in awe of these artistically creative people who seem to reap a double benefit from their hobby—freedom from tension and eventually a lovely finished product. If others can do it, so can I.

So at last I took the plunge, reasoning that everyone ought to have a "pass time" for a change of pace from normal responsibilities. I bought all the equipment, got some instruction, and bravely launched out.

It was anything but simple. Certainly it was not relaxing. I doubt that I have ever worked harder, that is until I began gradually to acquire a little dexterity and began to understand the hieroglyphics of the instructions. Suddenly it was fun! My dogged determination to master the art began to pay off when finally I could see the pattern begin to develop. By then I was "hooked"! I became so absorbed that I didn't want to quit and had to promise myself to knit just one more row before going to bed. That one more row led to another and another as the clock moved relentlessly past midnight.

Having repeated this several nights since I started the fiendish business, I have now called a halt for evaluation. It occurs to me that many things are being neglected in favor of the yarn and needles. Without realizing that it was happening, my "pass time" has started to kill time. It is usurping more and more time that rightly belongs to more essential projects. I don't need the sweater that is emerging, but finishing it has become an obsession.

This can happen with anything—particularly, I suppose, with a leisure-time activity. But when a pass time takes possession of a disproportionate share of time and interest, when it interferes with proper rest, when it takes a toll on health, then however good it is in itself, that good thing has become a bad thing.

Most of us recognize that time is a gift from God and that we have a stewardship responsibility for it as we do for his other gifts. It ought to be used wisely and well and we are held accountable for what we do with it.

The Phillips version of Eph. 5:16 says, "Make the best use of your time . . . ." To deliberately kill time is to destroy a gift of God, and surely this must be wrong.

But it is perhaps as wrong to take no time for personal recreation and renewal as it is to take too much so that health, rest, and productivity suffer as a result.

Moderation is, of course, the key to balanced living. Temperance, one of the fruits of the Spirit, should be exercised in both work and play.

I'm not going to quit knitting. It's a wonderful hobby, and I believe I need this type of switch from my daily work. But I am going to discipline myself so that it will serve its proper function of refreshment and strengthening for my work. I'm going to temper my enthusiasm with judgment and discretion.

Perhaps my undue absorption in knitting has

served one creative purpose: It made me evaluate the time it takes and the benefits it confers. Do you, perhaps, have a similar problem with temperate use of either your working or relaxing time?

Are You Maturing or Just Aging?

No one has yet figured out a way to avoid the relentless process of aging. Hour by hour, day by day, year by year, all of us are growing older. A doctor once said that he would not wish old age on even his worst enemy, but he could prescribe no cure.

Although aging is a natural phenomenon of life, we resist it and the constant changes it brings, possibly because we know it will ultimately lead to the grave. Besides the psychological aversion to aging, we fear the physical deterioration that comes with it. As age slows the step, disorients the coordination of mind and muscle, and makes our reflexes less dependable, the body begins to present one problem after another. Having been conditioned to the high premium that society places upon utility, we dread the time when our activity must be curtailed and we will be shelved as useless.

One elderly person said that those who praise old age have done so only when they were very young. But then she went on to say that a sane philosophy of age must start with the recognition that all periods of life have their differing values and difficulties. Individual dignity and worth need to be taken into consideration for people of all ages. To look backward continually, either in envy or to imitate youth, is to miss the glorious fact that right now you are living in the future of which you dreamed when you were younger. The present moment can be full and rich for anyone wise enough to know his limitations, to accept them and to fit his ambitions, occupations, and diversions sensibly to his age and agility at the time.

It is never easy to determine just exactly when youth slips into middle age or when middle age becomes frankly old age. However hard we cling to the youngest possible category, the time comes when we can no longer fool either the public or ourselves and we have to admit that we have graduated to the next level. Accepting the fact of our years is a mark of maturity.

When we were very young, people of forty seemed to be creaking antiques. But to those who are really old, forty seems a glowing, wonderfully young age that has promise of much active time ahead. Age is relative. How old we seem to each other depends on where we are standing and in which direction we are looking.

We are young only once, but unfortunately too many people remain immature indefinitely. There is not necessarily any relationship between chronological age and maturity. Some people who are very young in years evidence far more maturity in their attitudes than others who have lived a long time. The degree of maturity that has been achieved shows itself quite clearly in the way we rub off on one another in daily contact. Especially is this true when we are under pressure.

The mature person can usually maintain at least external poise in a tense situation. She is in control of herself, her emotions, and her actions. The immature person, however, to get her own way, or to avoid responsibility, or perhaps to punish someone else for a situation she finds difficult or embarrassing, may revert to some variation of the juvenile behavior pattern which brought the desired result in her childhood. She will use whatever weapon is handy to accomplish her ends. It may be a fit of temper, a burst of tears, a sullen, pouting silence. Sometimes the immature person needs to rebuild her faltering self-image so she will do this with big talk. She will brag about herself, her accomplishments, her possessions, her position—or even her more illustrious relatives! It is childish and embarrassing to others and it marks this adult as sadly immature. Certainly it adds nothing beneficial to her social relationships. The immature adult sees everything from the standpoint of how it affects her. She is not "big" enough emotionally to swallow her own disappointment or to sublimate her own desires in favor of the good of others or to bring harmony into a group.

The Apostle Paul defined maturity in Eph. 4:13 as a coming to the "fullness of Christ."

It is sad when an adult consistently shows marks of immaturity, for it is an indication that the old nature is still in possession of her life. Although we do not ever arrive at full maturity in this life, day by day we ought to be growing in the fullness of Christ, becoming more like him.

Although we may continue to take a dim view of the dubious merits of growing old, it is nothing to fear or to resist if at the same time we are maturing in the sense that we are becoming more

Christ-like. Then old age is progression in the direction of perfection instead of toward deterioration and decay.

We will continue to add one year after another, but if, as adults, we continue to act like spoiled children, we have ceased to mature. We are not growing in the fullness of Christ. We can expect no end of difficulty in our relationships with one another and very little satisfaction with ourselves.

It is not enough simply to age. We must also mature. This comes day by day as we let our Lord Jesus Christ guide and direct us so that we can meet life's problems and every encounter with our fellowmen in an unselfish consideration of their rights and privileges. Then we will not simply grow tall, we will grow up and mature as Christian adults should!

A Woman Is a Many-Splendored Thing!

What is a woman?

There are as many answers to that question as there are women. Each is a distinct personality with individual characteristics—some good, some bad—but all are marvelously complex creatures with tremendous potential.

Disraeli, British author, once bitterly stated that "the only useless life is woman's." Earlier Euripides, tragic dramatist of ancient Greece, wrote, "There is no evil so terrible as a woman." Such caustic comments can have sprung only from an unhappy personal encounter that at least momentarily blinded these men to many desirable qualities that even the least observant recognize in woman generally.

The Danish philosopher Søren Kierkegaard, whose conclusions in matters of the spirit have influenced the thinking of many eminent scholars, once wrote, "To be a woman is something so strange, so confused, so complicated that only a woman could put up with it."

Long gone is the concept that woman is a fragile flower always to be protected. Perhaps Kierkegaard put his finger on a truth when he pointed out the hardiness of woman who can endure even the severe trial of being a woman! There is a tough resiliency in the fiber of woman that can bend, stretch, and be pulled well beyond the breaking point and still spring back to tackle the next go-round that life hands her. One explanation of this may be the tears which a woman uses to release pent-up emotion. Shedding a few tears makes her capable of "taking it." Although tears may cause some "soul erosion," at the same time they also moisturize it and keep it flexible so that it doesn't break under pressure.

Recently a man with whom I was doing business said, "I can talk to you like a man." He meant it as a compliment, but I was not pleased, for it seemed to discredit my femininity. What he meant, no doubt, was that he believed I would face up to the situation objectively and without emotion. What he didn't know—for I believe I concealed it well—was that at the moment he made that statement I could feel my heart sinking and tears rising to the lids as I saw my carefully drawn suggestions being swept aside by a few well-meant strokes of masculine efficiency!

As a business woman, however, I have learned to control the tendency to let feelings govern my decisions. Women in business constantly meet men on what must be acknowledged to be "their ground." Thus, while retaining our femininity as far as possible, we must adopt their weapons. We must be calm, give a fair hearing to all sides of a question, and then render a decision that is based on cold, hard fact rather than emotion. (Women dealing with each other can arrive at exactly the same conclusions in less time simply by employing that marvelous feminine faculty of intuition!)

Woman is a limitless person who adapts to the need that confronts her. She has many careers, most of which she never intended to pursue, but which have been forced upon her by the simple expedient of her family's welfare. Most young girls in their romantic dreams of the future do not see themselves as what most housewives and mothers ultimately become: cook, laundress, chauffeur, arbiter in disputes, nurse, gardener, interior decorator, seamstress, teacher, psychologist, and disciplinarian. But there is happiness for the woman who finds satisfaction in being all things to her family and the heart and core around which the home revolves.

What is woman? She is a many-splendored thing who must rediscover the ancient wisdom that her greatest happiness will come from being completely, gladly feminine in whatever way she has been called to live out her life—even in business!

Do You Care Enough?

"When you care enough to send the very best" —this familiar slogan of a greeting card firm implies superior quality in their stock sentiments to express your deepest feeling on special occasions.

The fabulous growth of the greeting card business is in itself an indictment—we obviously don't care enough even to say it in our own words!

All of us are subject to a certain degree of laziness which explains our taking the easy way out. Then, too, we attempt to maintain many contacts when our lives are already full of many things to do. There are, no doubt, other legitimate reasons for our mass swing to mechanical expression of our love.

However, there is something more serious than occasional greetings on special days involved.

Being sensitive to the reaction of others (even those we would like to help), we sometimes become shy and reserved, afraid to expose our feelings when we care the most. Fearing possible ridicule or laughter, we gulp back the sympathetic words we might have spoken; we swallow the tears of compassion we might have shed; we squelch the impulse to do a kind deed. We may be moved enough, however, to hie ourselves off to the nearest card shop, buy a quarter's worth of "canned" sentiment and dispatch it by mail. Thus we avoid the risk of letting our feelings show or becoming personally involved, and at the same time we salve our consciences by having done *something*.

Jesus in his earthly ministry issued just one commandment, and it dealt with our love for one another: "The commandments . . . are summed up in this sentence 'You shall love your neighbor as yourself.' "

Notice that his commandment indicates the character of that love: ". . . as yourself."

If we are normally sane, we will provide our own food, clothing, and shelter; we will spare ourselves pain and suffering; we will make ourselves as comfortable and happy as possible. That is how we love ourselves.

The commandment of Jesus puts down these very same specifications for love toward our neighbor. To love him "as ourselves" means that we must have a similar concern for his needs.

There are times when a well-expressed sentiment means a great deal, but words alone—whether our own or on a printed card—are scant evidence of Christian concern where a neighbor has an obvious need for our help. Whether we like him or not, God has made him our concern.

To love our neighbor as ourselves is God's command, but real love has a better motivation: we love because God has first loved us.

Do we care enough if we discharge our responsibility with a greeting card and ignore a need for *us*?

She Ran Quickly

It wasn't quite dawn when she arrived, but there was light enough to see that something was not entirely right.

She had expected guards—but they were gone.

She had wondered about the stone—but it was rolled back, exposing the gaping, black entrance.

There was something more, something about the atmosphere itself—it seemed electric, suspended in time.

But she didn't panic.

Only a few years ago she would have. Now, however, she was poised, unafraid, as only one with complete inner calm can be. She was no longer a neurotic, seeing threats in every shadow.

She was whole—a whole new woman. Terrors no longer haunted her by night. She could sleep and awake refreshed as she had this morning, eager to be about the day's tasks.

It had been an emotionally exhausting weekend. A friend who was also her physician and teacher had died, destroyed in the prime of life by a mob who certainly must have misunderstood him. His ideas were indeed revolutionary. Only close friends seemed to catch the meaning of his teaching. But what could possibly be wrong with a philosophy based entirely on an utterly selfless love?

She came before daylight to pay her last respects to a friend, but he was not there! In tenderhearted woman fashion, she began to cry.

"Woman, why weepest thou?" The question came from a man she thought was the gardener.

She was explaining the disappearance of the body of her friend, when the man spoke a single word—her own name: "Mary."

It was enough. In that instant she recognized him and knew him to be the Son of God, the long-expected Savior.

She, who had been neurotic (possessed of seven devils), knew the miraculous healing power of God. She had served Jesus in his life; she had ministered to him in his suffering and death; she was permitted to witness his resurrection; and equipped with the most important asset: recognition of his divinity, she was the first one sent forth with his triumphant message.

And as all must who have been healed, who have recognized their Lord, who have been told to "Go . . . tell"—Mary ran *quickly*!

Christmas Was a Disappointment

That year Christmas was a disappointment—or rather my gifts were. For most children presents are the most important part of Christmas and many times they bring as much unhappiness as joy.

I had my heart set on a bright, red scooter in the local hardware store. Early in December I began an organized campaign of hinting. One by one I paraded members of my family through the store, calling attention to the superior qualities of the coveted toy. The acme of happiness, it seemed to me, would be to propel myself down the sidewalk on this gleaming, two-wheeled vehicle which was so enticing. But my family had their own ideas.

Christmas Eve there was a spectacular array of gifts for me—a doll with real hair and jointed arms and legs, a buggy, a doll bed, a complete wardrobe of handmade clothes for the doll. I should have been jubilant, but I was disappointed and unhappy, perhaps as much from being ashamed of my ingratitude as from the subconscious resentment that my family had been too preoccupied with what they thought I ought to want to sense what I really wanted. However, they were obviously so thrilled over the generous gifts that I didn't want them to know how I felt, so I swallowed hard and feigned an enthusiasm that I didn't really feel.

Admittedly I was a spoiled child, but who of us, even as adults, has not experienced some measure of disappointment when a gift has not measured up to our expectations? Who has not been unhappy when a longed-for treasure failed to satisfy the deep desire that had reached fever pitch before it became a reality? Even what we think we can hardly live without can be a letdown when we finally get it.

To be perfectly honest, we all like to get gifts,

especially when someone has been sensitive enough to our needs and desires to choose something just to please us. It tells us someone has cared enough to make the effort. We all consider our own birthday as a special day, not because we add another year to our accumulation, but because being the birthday child focuses attention upon us and we secretly hope for little surprise gifts.

The universal desire for gifts is actually a deep need for acceptance and for proof of esteem. Our desire is not so much for the gift itself or the pleasure we expect to get from it as for the affection of which it is a symbol. Even the person who "has everything, including a bag to put it in" needs an occasional surprise gift that has been selected especially for him as evidence that someone likes him.

But unfortunately there is nothing really permanent about gifts—even the most carefully chosen ones. They can be lost, or broken, or worn out. We need constant renewal of the symbol, constant reassurance of the love they are meant to express, more, bigger, and better gifts. And still there is an emptiness within us because it is not the gift we really want—it is the giver; not the *thing* but the *person*.

God gives his gifts generously and indiscriminately. He lavishes them upon all his creatures. His gifts are all around us. They are extravagant evidences of his bounty. We may not see them as symbols of his love. We may simply take them for granted as our just due. But even when we do recognize the goodness and unstinting generosity of a benevolent Father-God, his gifts don't really satisfy us either. There is still within each of us a deep, indefinable longing for something more.

As human beings we need assurance of a love that lasts—an absolute, unchanging, dependable love. Our desire for gifts is "nothing other than a seeking after God," says Paul Tournier, the Swiss physician and psychotherapist. "At the point of death, the only one which can be unchanging in value is the assurance of life beyond the grave." This is an echo of what the Apostle Paul wrote to the Romans, ". . . *the free gift of God is eternal life in Christ Jesus our Lord.*"

Tournier continues, "The great gift, the unique and living one, is not a thing but a person. It is Jesus Christ himself. In him God has given himself, no longer just things which he creates or has created but his own person, his own suffering, his own solitude given unto death itself."

In God's gifts we touch his hand, but in Christ

we receive him: his heart, spirit, mind, and will. Christmas gifts are symbols of God's great Gift and the love that prompted it. As such they have great value, but they cannot be an end in themselves.

The deep yearning that becomes particularly poignant at Christmas is our need for God. We were created for fellowship with him and we will be empty, disappointed, and dissatisfied until we are reconciled.

Ecumenicity

When I rang the bell at the Methodist Church, I had never heard the word "ecumenicity." Of course, I was only six years old at the time, so perhaps it is not strange that I hadn't yet added it to my vocabulary.

It is a word that we are beginning to use more and more these days. The dictionary says it means "universal" or "all-inclusive." For too long the churches have been exclusive. We have each built our own denominational walls higher and higher. But now in the last few years we are beginning to be more ecumenical. We are putting a few gates in our walls. We are cautiously beginning to talk to one another. We are entering into what the theologians call "dialogue." And wonder of wonders, we are discovering that we have a great deal in common—the most important things, such as the same human needs and the same Lord Jesus Christ.

The children in my home town knew that many years ago. Perhaps children in some small communities tend to be more ecumenical simply because they know each other so well from attending the same public school and skating at the same rink. It was only on Sunday morning for worship services and Sunday school that we were segregated by denomination. Otherwise we were very ecumenical. We carried on continual dialogues about many things; and quite often it was about our faith. We knew we had a great deal in common. We enjoyed our interdenominational fellowship and wandered freely in and out of each other's churches whenever there was something interesting going on.

We didn't miss a Christmas program in any of the churches. Of course, the fact that every child was given a sack of hard candy may have had something to do with it. We liked to go to the Presbyterian Church because they had a sand table in the basement where we could mold the

damp sand into the little town of Bethlehem and
stock it with tiny camels and sheep. We went to
the Epworth League at the Methodist Church on
Sunday afternoon, partly because there was nothing else to do, but also because they gave prizes
for Bible memorization.

It was for a perfect recitation of the Beatitudes
from Jesus' Sermon on the Mount that I got a
chance to ring the bell. Competition for the privilege was keen and we studied hard to earn it. The
fact that I was a Lutheran was not held against me.

A heavy rope with several huge knots in it dan-
gled from the bell tower, just out of reach. It required an agile leap into the air to grasp the rope
just above one of the knots for a firm grip. Then
the trick was to bend your knees and sink slowly
toward the floor, letting your body weight swing
the huge bell as far as it would go in one direction. The big clapper would fall with a resounding
"ding!" As the momentum would swing the bell
far to the other limit of its arc, the whole tower
would quiver. The child hanging onto the rope
would be lifted high into the air for the answering
"dong!" There was just no thrill like it! The free
ride on the end of the bell rope was so much fun
that the adult adviser had to strictly limit the num-

ber of dings and dongs per child. We relinquished
the rope with great reluctance.

We memorized huge portions of Scripture and
earned celluloid book marks and tiny gold cross
lapel pins for it. Ringing the bell was the top
award. We learned a lot of Scripture in the process. Our common denominator was the Bible. The
very same Jesus we knew and loved from our own
Sunday school was taught in each of the meetings
we attended.

Very early we discovered there were some basic
differences between the churches. Some churches
didn't have an altar. Some had baptismal fonts for
sprinkling and some had big tanks beneath sliding
panels for immersion. We compared notes and
learned that some of us would have to "read for
the minister" and be confirmed at about the age
of 15. Some would not even be baptized until
they were almost that old. This didn't bother us.
We respected these differences and accepted
them without question. We just concentrated on
memorizing the Bible.

God's love is universal. It is all-inclusive. It is
ecumenical. The Scriptures encourage us to scale
the walls which have shut us away from each
other. It can open our eyes to human suffering

and need, and it suggests that we should respond with deeds of Christ-like love without asking for credentials or appreciation. When we see how indiscriminately God loves all his children, we ought to have concluded that "If God so loved us, we also ought to love one another."

Realizing that there are some basic and important doctrinal differences that have not been resolved, we can, nevertheless, concentrate on what we have in common. In our local communities, if we obey the command to love, we can share our faith in Jesus and our knowledge and respect for his holy Word. It may require an agile leap to get a good grip on the rope, but if we make the effort, we may experience the thrill of ringing ecumenical bells in heaven. Surely there are no denominational walls there!

Who Is Indispensable?

With a stick I wrote my name in huge letters in the smooth, white sand by Lake Michigan. Almost immediately a wave rolled in and completely obliterated the signature. The beach was firm, white, and unmarked when the water receded, leaving no vestige of my sand-writing.

It was as ego-deflating as the occasional thought that we can pass through this life and leave a scarcely discernible mark upon it.

We have seen hard-working, dedicated people drop by the wayside, become incapacitated, or die in the midst of what had been for them an all-consuming project. It is sobering and somewhat frightening to see how quickly someone else is able to pick up and carry on a task we had thought no one else could do.

Though we may feel that we are the only one for a particular job, the facts are not in our favor. In most instances we can easily, quickly (and perhaps better) be replaced.

This may be the subconscious reason for our hesitation to "lay down the hammer" and take a rest although aching muscles and tired minds cry out for relief.

God set a pattern for the worker when he created the world. He labored in that important occupation for six days. On the seventh day he rested.

To push the body and mind beyond normal limits, even in the most necessary work, is sin. It is gross waste when a good workman collapses from overwork when properly spaced periods of change and relaxation might have prevented total incapacity.

It is not easy to take time for rest when pressures pound relentlessly upon us, but no one can continue indefinitely at peak efficiency unless a sensibly spaced "breather" provides an opportunity for change of pace, relaxation, and recovery of strength for a fresh start.

James wrote: "Come now, you who say, 'Today or tomorrow we will go into such and such a town and spend a year there and trade and get gain'; whereas you do not know about tomorrow. What is your life? For you are a mist that appears for a little time and then vanishes. Instead you ought to say, 'If the Lord wills, we shall live and we shall do this or that.' As it is, you boast in your arrogance. All such boasting is evil. Whoever knows what is right to do and fails to do it, for him it is sin" (James 4:13-17).

The Word of God calls us arrogant—we who think we are so indispensable that we can ignore the stewardship of our minds and bodies. These are the most precious gifts God has given—life and health, strength and ability. Should we then be prodigal in their use? We are also called sinners—we who know what is right and fail to do it!

Who is indispensable? No one, really. We can do our best when we have accepted that fact and live accordingly.

Me and My Big Mouth!

"Me and my big mouth! We did it again!"

I could kick myself for what I said, but that wouldn't wipe the hurt look from my friend's face. I said it, and now it is out there in the big world, beyond my recall. I didn't mean to say it—it just somehow slipped out.

"Me and my big mouth!" I say in disgust and self-loathing. It's not a very adequate apology. It won't erase what I said. It doesn't excuse my loose lips and undisciplined tongue.

Gripped by the enormity of what my uncontrolled words have done, I can understand a little better how Isaiah felt when he cried out, "Woe is me! For I am lost; I am a man of unclean lips!"

I know now what James meant when he wrote, "The human tongue is physically small but what tremendous effects it can boast of! A whole forest can be set ablaze by a tiny spark of fire, and the tongue is as dangerous as any fire with vast potentialities for evil. It can poison the whole body, it can make the whole of life a blazing hell."

Just a few carelessly spoken words have put me in a most embarrassing position. They have jeopardized a friendship and caused a deep wound that may never entirely be healed.

That little tongue that each of us has can get us into trouble so easily. Perhaps it spews out gossip, slander, or accusations. Or it may criticize, belittle, or abuse. Sometimes it is even so malicious as to ridicule, to be profane, to tell a salacious story, or to violate a confidence. Truly the tongue is a "restless evil, full of deadly poison," as James said. "With it we bless the Lord and Father, and with it we curse men, who are made in the likeness of God. From the same mouth come blessing and cursing." Obviously the tongue is a member of the body that needs firm control!

I realize from Jesus' words that the effect of idle talk is even more long-range than I had thought. He said, "On the day of judgment men will render account for every careless word they utter." Even "death and life are in the power of the tongue," it says in Proverbs 18:21. This is more serious than I thought! Me and my big mouth have really put me in a bad spot this time!

So I search the Word for some reassurance—

and I find a little. James wrote it. "We all make mistakes in all kinds of ways . . . [I feel better already] . . . but the man who can claim that he never says the wrong thing can consider himself perfect, for if he can control his tongue he can control every part of his personality!"

There is some comfort in that—but not enough. I know I am not perfect. I know that I can't control my tongue. I know that I can't stop the raging forest fire that my careless words have already started. I need help. James makes another suggestion, "If any of you is in trouble let him pray."

So I ask God to forgive me, to help me repair the damage already done, and I voice the words I found in Psalm 141:3—"Set a guard over my mouth, O Lord, keep watch over the door of my lips!"

We Would See Jesus

The photographer provided six proofs from which to choose the portrait he was to make for me. I quickly discarded one on which the camera had caught me with one eye shut and another on which I seemed to be suffering an acute pain. But

I couldn't decide among the others, so I asked a few close friends to help me select one.

Everyone who looked at them had a different reaction. One hesitantly commented, "The lighting is very good—" One said, "Ugh! None of these looks like you!" Another hedged, "Well, maybe, if the photographer could touch up your nose—" One friend (bless her heart!) said, "You're much prettier than your picture."

They weren't much help. None really liked any of the proofs. It made me wonder: What do I really look like to these people? I had thought the proofs were pretty good likenesses. The thought occurred, perhaps these friends who know me so well don't really see me when they look at me. It is possible that each of them sees me as each of them knows me, and their concept of my appearance may be something other than a camera would record.

Perhaps it is impossible accurately to describe the physical appearance of someone we know very well or whom we hold especially dear. It is not easy to separate objectively what we see when we look at such a person from how we know him to be as a human personality from our experiences with him.

This may explain why none of the detailed

records of the life and work of Jesus made by his close friends in the Gospels includes a real description of his personal appearance. The only reference to how he looked that I could find was what Matthew wrote when he was dazzled by the transfiguration: "His face shone like the sun and his garments became white as light."

The appearance of Jesus has tantalized the imagination of artists, poets, and writers for a thousand years—and perhaps it has defeated them all. Really none of us knows what he looks like. The mental image that each of us carries is strongly influenced by the kind of drawings we saw in our early Sunday school books and the pictures we had in our homes. The portraits of Jesus with which we are familiar range all the way from sentimental, almost effeminate, beauty to stark ugliness. They show him as placid, meek, mild, suffering, vindictive, and even grotesque. When we see pictures of Jesus we react in many different ways. If Jesus has special meaning to us, we are likely to be emotional in our reaction. How we know him; what he means to us; whether we love him, fear him, resent him, discredit him, revere him, or reject him—all these things enter into our judgment. An artist, unlike a camera, creates out of his own imagination and out of his personal knowledge of the subject. His experience with Jesus may be something entirely other than that of the people who see his work. Yet we tend to evaluate the relative merits of a painting of Jesus on the basis of our own emotional experience.

The prophecies in Isaiah give some information about the appearance of Jesus that do not suggest beauty. In Isaiah 52 it says, "As many were astonished at him—his appearance was so marred, beyond human semblance, and his form beyond that of the sons of men—" In the next chapter, this is amplified, "He had no form or comeliness that we should look at him, and no beauty that we should desire him."

The writer of Hebrews said, "He reflects the glory of God and bears the very stamp of his nature." His dual nature is described in the Philippians reference which speaks of his being "in the form of God" and taking "the form of a servant" when he was "born in the likeness of man."

The sparsity of physical description suggests that it is more important that we know who he is than how he looks. He was attractive, but not in the sense that he was irresistibly handsome. His attraction is such that, as he said of himself, "I, when I am lifted up from the earth will draw all men to myself."

Philippians puts its emphasis on the name of Jesus. "God has bestowed on him the name which is above every name, that at the name of Jesus every knee should bow, in heaven and on earth and under the earth, and every tongue confess that Jesus Christ is Lord, to the glory of God the Father."

Like the Greeks who exclaimed, "We would see Jesus!" we wish we could know everything about him, including exactly how he looks—but we don't need to know that, for "Blessed are they who have not seen and yet have believed."

Blessing in Mourning

The young man addressing the crowd on the hillside was obviously a radical, for who else would say things that so completely contradict common sense?

Everyone knows, of course, that if you are going to be happy, you need plenty of money, everything should run smoothly, you should be surrounded by compatible people, and you must be completely free from troubles or sorrow.

Yet Jesus equated blessedness (or happiness) with such things as being poor in spirit, with being hungry and thirsty for righteousness, with being meek and persecuted. He even went so far as to say, "Blessed are those who mourn, for they shall be comforted." So much of what he taught and expected people to believe reversed what we have always cherished as the way of life. His thinking and ours are often completely at odds.

It is difficult, for instance, to see any good in mourning. It is a crushing, debilitating experience that drains life of all meaning and leaves one limp and exhausted. Certainly to try to squeeze happiness out of it seems ridiculous. But if we have had the courage to take Jesus at his word in other matters, we have learned that he never spoke idle words. He meant what he said. Everything he said is truth. His way of life *can* be lived, although it may take a good measure of the grace of God and considerable personal fortitude to face up to life's more trying situations with his kind of philosophy which sees blessing in adversity. Strange as it may seem on the surface, however, what Jesus advocated is always for our ultimate good. It usually results in the betterment of mankind in general and brings glory to God. But how is it possible to find blessing in mourning?

The very fact that we are subject to deep sorrow and mourning indicates that we are not entirely self-sufficient. When we have plunged to the depths of despair, we don't feel very sure of ourselves or very capable of mastering our own destiny. The bottom drops out of life. There is an acute sense of futility and an aching loneliness. We realize that we have come to the end of ourselves and of our resources.

Here may be the first glimmer of what Jesus meant when he said there is blessing in mourning. When the props have been knocked out from under us and we find ourselves unable to depend on our pride, power, possessions, and all the other things that normally sustain us, then God can reach us. He can lift us up and comfort us. Some of us, unfortunately, need to be reduced to this state of complete helplessness before we will acknowledge God and reach out and grasp the hand he offers. If this is the result of mourning, then it can be a blessed state. There can be blessing and real joy only when God pours out his healing, grace, love, and hope upon us and we accept it with eager, open hands.

Another possible blessing of mourning is that it qualifies us to comfort others. In 2 Cor. 1:3-4, Paul spoke of God as the "God of all comfort, who comforts us in our affliction, so that we may be able to comfort those who are in any affliction, with the comfort with which we ourselves were comforted." If we haven't known the comfort of God, we can't properly transmit it to others. We are ready for the task if we know from our own experience what it means to reach the depths and to have received God's strength to endure and to carry on. What we have learned of the grace, mercy, and love of God can be shared. This, too, is blessed.

Often we sympathize with those who mourn, but we don't bring them real comfort. There is a difference between sympathy and comfort according to the root meanings of the two words. "To sympathize" is "to feel with" or to experience the same human emotion. On the other hand, "to comfort" is "to give strength."

One who mourns appreciates that someone feels with him and shares his weeping, but it means considerably more if the sympathizer can also bring strength to help the mourner to endure and to carry on. The comfort that Christians bring to one another ought to be the assurance of the love and the hope of Christ.

One of the Old Testament prophecies speaks of Christ in this manner, "The Lord has appointed me to bring good tidings to the afflicted . . . to comfort all who mourn" (Isa. 61:1-2). Jesus is the one who comforts.

There will be times of weeping, but as the Psalmist wrote, "Weeping may tarry for the night, but joy comes with the morning." The God of *all* comfort is always there, ready to help. He sympathizes with us because he knows our weakness, understands our nature, and feels our hurts. But he also imparts his strength to pick ourselves up, his wisdom to determine what we must do next, his patience to wait for things to work out, his faith to believe that "in everything God works for good with those who love him" (Rom. 8:28), and his hope that "does not disappoint us, because God's love has been poured into our hearts through the Holy Spirit which has been given to us" (Rom. 5:5).

There is blessing—and even happiness—inherent in mourning, for comfort is available in Christ who brings so much more than sympathy. He brings new life to all who receive him. It becomes an opportunity for Christ to bring sympathy, comfort, and new life to all who will admit him to their hours of sorrow.

What Gets Your Goat?

What does it take to "get your goat"? Not much sometimes! Anger flares up within us over little things so easily!

Sometimes we even take a kind of perverse pride in our anger. We say, "It made me so mad! I was absolutely furious!" We actually seem to boast about the intensity of our emotional outburst as though there were some merit in being able to produce a particularly high-grade rage. We speak of our anger as though it were an amiable weakness that only makes us seem more human. And in a sense it does this, for perhaps nothing is more common to natural man than the way he reacts to irritants.

We resent having our movement restrained. We are quickly irritated when we are slowed down, held back, or have our progress in any way impeded. An obvious example is the driver of a car who is forced to stay behind a slow-moving truck. Another source of this kind of annoyance may be a clerk who dawdles, making small talk with another clerk while you wait for service. A clerk may be equally irritated by a customer who can't make a decision and keeps others waiting while he monopolizes the clerk's attention.

Sometimes we even take out our animosity upon inanimate things that thwart us. For example, we may slam the door of a car that won't start or become so angry over a bad shot that we will smash a golf club against a tree.

We get angry when we are treated with condescension or disdain. We all have a pretty high opinion of ourselves, and anger flares almost involuntarily when someone indicates by word or deed that we are less than we think we are. That's why criticism (especially when it is deserved) tends to make us angry. Wounded vanity mistakenly seeks healing in anger only to find that anger never heals, it only spreads the infection. When injured pride lashes out in fury it leaves us with much less of which to be proud. We are always diminished in the eyes of others when we lose control of ourselves.

None of us likes to be imposed upon. Any infringement upon what we consider to be our rights arouses ire within us. We don't want anyone to get ahead of us in a line, or to cut in on our time, or to usurp what we consider to be our special privileges. It irritates us to have anyone

trespass on what we have staked out as our particular domain. It irks us to be short-changed in a
business transaction. We are highly incensed if we
discover that goods we have purchased have been
misrepresented. We expect fair play and honest
measure or we feel quite justified in becoming
angry. Unfortunately, we are not normally so concerned about justice and fair play for others.

If we could consciously recall the emotional
experience and make a detailed analysis of the
provocation, how we reacted to it, and what actually was accomplished by giving way to anger,
we would be ashamed to realize how childish,
irrational, and ridiculous it all was. Often the
things that arouse our anger are not worthy of the
importance our temper tantrums give them. What
a nasty emotion anger is! And what a devastating
effect it has upon us and upon the regard that
others have for us!

The Book of Proverbs indicates that it is the
better part of wisdom to control our tempers:

"A fool gives full vent to his anger, but a wise
man quietly holds it back" (Prov. 29:11). "Good
sense makes a man slow to anger and it is his glory
to overlook an offense" (Prov. 19:11).

Jesus put anger in its proper perspective in his
Sermon on the Mount when he equated it with

murder, "Whoever kills shall be liable to judgment. But I say to you that everyone who is angry with his brother shall be liable to judgment."

Paul, in outlining for the Colossians what belongs to the old life of sin and the new life in Christ, said, "Put them all away: anger, wrath, malice, slander and foul talk from your mouth" (Col. 3:8), and he continued, "Put on then, as God's chosen ones, holy and beloved, compassion, kindness, lowliness, meekness, and patience, forbearing one another and, if one has a complaint against another, forgiving each other; as the Lord has forgiven you, so you also must forgive" (Col. 3:12-13).

Paul's suggestion is that we do something concrete about the nasty emotion of anger: replace it with one of the better emotions such as compassion, kindness, lowliness, patience, forgiveness. This is a very sound psychological principle of reconditioning whereby one substitutes or attaches a new emotion to the same situation. This is how one "overcomes evil by doing good," as Paul told the Romans they must do.

Certainly Jesus could have been provoked to anger by the way he was treated. He was blocked in his progress of teaching, healing, ministering to the needs of people after only three short years

He was demeaned, insulted, and subjected to all manner of personal humiliation. He suffered the most gross injustice. Yet his reaction was not as ours might be under similar circumstances. He was filled with compassion and he asked only that his tormentors be forgiven.

Paul continued in his Letter to the Colossians, "*let* the peace of Christ rule in your hearts . . . and *let* the Word of Christ dwell in you richly . . . And above all these put on love which binds everything together in perfect harmony."

If all we do in word or deed is done in the name of the Lord Jesus and in his spirit, and if we give thanks through him to God the Father, it will take much more than trivialities to "get our goat"!